The Witnessing Community

THE *Witnessing Community*

The Biblical Record of God's Purpose

by

SUZANNE DE DIETRICH

The Westminster Press
Philadelphia

Library of Congress Catalog Card No. 58–5020

PRINTED IN THE UNITED STATES OF AMERICA

Contents

Foreword

Protestantism lives on the conviction that the Bible is the people's book. The Reformation put the Scriptures into the hands of laymen, and a smoldering faith burst into flame. A strange quirk of history, however, conspired to take the Bible away from laymen by the very movement that began in an effort to give it to them. The rise of critical study, with its demand for specialization in so many fields, tended to restrict the study of the Bible to the clergy and professional students of religion. Thus, once more the layman's knowledge of the Bible became limited to that which he received secondhand from others.

One of the marks of the present time is Protestantism's awakening awareness that the results of specialized study of the Bible must somehow be mediated to laymen, whose major time is of necessity given to carrying on the work of the world. There is appearing, therefore, a spate of books designed to capture the attention of the lay mind. Some of these talk down to the layman in a fashion unworthy of serious consideration. Some tell him the wrong things. It is difficult to combine serious study of the Bible, reflecting the results of specialized study, with a type of presentation that is at once understandable and challenging.

Here is a work that brings these into happy combination. Suzanne de Dietrich has been endowed, both by training and by experience, with the ability to speak to the lay mind. Trained originally in the field of advanced engineering, she has an analytical type of mind which sees immediately to the heart of issues and states them succinctly and clearly. For long years she has taught the Bible to student groups of many nations and to

9

varied groups of professional laymen. Her work in connection with the Ecumenical Institute at Bossey, Switzerland, has given her opportunity to work with all sorts of laymen, from all walks of life, from all branches of the church, from all over the world. The breadth of her experience and outlook, limited only by her supreme devotion to the evangelical faith, is clearly reflected within the pages of this book. The Biblical faith of which she writes is congenial to her because she has wrought out her understanding of it on the anvil of suffering. The rewriting of this book was undertaken during a long period of pain and discomfort resulting from an accident. For this reason, the Biblical message is to her more than an abstract theology — it is a living word on the way of life, when the going is hard.

Considered by many to be the outstanding lay theologian of Europe, Suzanne de Dietrich has been honored by the great and loved by the humble. She has written extensively in her mother tongue, French, which writings have been translated into other languages. She has written articles in English for religious periodicals, and some years ago wrote a work on the Bible published in England under the title *Rediscovering the Bible*.

It is an honor to introduce this present work, written in English by the author. Those who have assisted in preparing it for publication have sought to leave the characteristic freshness of the author's language untouched. A serious reading of this work by either ministers or laymen will make the history of the People of God more real and meaningful, will bring home the contemporary relevance of the Bible with freshness and power, and will stimulate lines of study that will carry one quite beyond the limits of this one volume.

DONALD G. MILLER

Union Theological Seminary
Richmond, Virginia

Preface

The materials of this book were first delivered as a series of lectures to the students of Union Theological Seminary in Richmond, Virginia, in the spring of 1955, while I was privileged to be a visiting professor in that institution. Since that time, extensive revisions have been made in both their form and content. They are offered now to a wider public in the hope that they will aid the readers to understand the fundamental unity that underlies God's dealings with his people through the Biblical period, and to see the relevance of the Biblical record to the life of the church in the world today.

My thanks go to Professor Donald G. Miller of Union Theological Seminary in Richmond, Virginia, for editing the manuscript of this book for the press, to his colleague Professor Frank Bell Lewis who, without altering the general tone of my own writing, made many stylistic improvements, and to Mr. Connolly Gamble, who read and corrected proof. I wish also to extend my gratitude to the Parishfield Community in Brighton, Michigan, whose hospitality and help I enjoyed while rewriting the manuscript.

SUZANNE DE DIETRICH

Paris, France

Introduction

A book appeared a few years ago under the significant title *The Lonely Crowd*, by David Riesman and others (Yale University Press, 1953). Modern man lives in crowded cities buzzing with life. Yet never has he been more lonely. In the farm or workshop of old, the wife and children could share in the tasks and concerns of the father of the house. Furthermore, one knew one's neighbors. Now, these natural communities — the family, the village, the neighborhood — are either nonexistent or subject to a centrifugal force which drives the members apart. One's place of work is distant from one's home. Each member of the family lives his own life, has his own circle of interests and acquaintances. He goes to his club or his trade-union. He turns on his television. The spiritual void remains.

There is today, everywhere, a hunger and thirst for "community." What "community" means is not always clear. We react against the individualistic tendencies that so deeply marked both secular and religious society in the West during the nineteenth century. But the search for fellowship can easily take superficial and questionable forms. It can become an escape from personal decision and responsibility. It can lead to mass psychology and dictatorship. The rights of the person as a person tend to be sacrificed to the so-called interests of the group, whether the group is class, nation, or race.

Our firm belief is that it is part of the calling of the church to show the world what true community means: a fellowship of free persons bound to one another by a common calling and a common service. Only in Christ can we solve the tension between freedom and authority, between the right of the individual person to attain fullness of life and the claim of the community as a whole on each of its members. For in and through him we learn what it means to be perfectly free, yet obedient unto death; to come as a servant, yet through this very self-abasement to attain fullness of life.

We must, therefore, ask ourselves the questions: How far is the local congregation, how far is the church as a whole, this exemplary fellowship which by its very existence should be a constant challenge to the world? How can we help to heal the strife and tensions of the world, if the same divisions and tensions exist in our midst?

We are called upon constantly to rethink our vocation as God's People, called upon to manifest in word and deed the work of reconciliation already achieved in Christ. It seems to be the distinctive gift of the Spirit to the church in this century that there is a greater awareness of the corporate and dynamic character of Christian witness. The very existence of the ecumenical movement bears testimony to this inward need for renewal and for unity.

The present book would like to be a small contribution to this common search. It tries to start from the Biblical revelation as it unfolds itself in history, so that we may see more clearly what it means to belong to God's People in our own day.

The Bible presents us with a *body of witnesses:* Israel and the apostolic church. A single man may be at a given moment the spokesman or the true embodiment of the group. But he never stands alone; he carries a message that is meant for the community to which he belongs or that will call a new community into being. In other words, all through the Biblical records, the Word of God *builds community*. Conversely we may say that Israel, or the church, is the fellowship of those who have *heard* and *believed*. Past deeds of God are told, recorded, interpreted, and proclaimed generation after generation in the context of a living, ongoing relationship with that same living God " who spoke to our fathers." They are told, recorded, interpreted so that the present generation may hearken and believe. There is a succession of the faith running through the Bible (see Heb., chs. 11; 12). Because the God of the Bible acts in and through history, we find frequent recapitulations of his past deeds; and each recapitulation, bearing the marks of the time in which it is made, aims at a specific purpose: the conversion or the strengthening of the community to which this Word of God is preached. Thus the Bible never faces us with bare events, but rather with a proclamation of these events by the community that lives them and is conscious of having been shaped by them — more, of owing its very existence to them.

It is the certainty that God called their fathers, that his mighty hand delivered the captive tribes from the yoke of Egypt, that makes a herd of slaves into a People, the covenanted People of God. It is the certainty that Jesus of Nazareth, crucified under Pontius Pilate, is risen from the dead, and the certainty of the Pentecost event, that makes a group of disheartened disciples into a living church. In both cases the immediate result of God's redeeming action is the coming into being of a community, a fellowship of believers.

There is no external proof that the testimony of these witnesses is *true*. All we can see is a peculiar people, standing in the stream of history, proclaiming with impassioned conviction through its prophets and apostles that there is a living God at work in history, a God standing over us in mercy and in judgment, coming finally into our midst as the Word made flesh, and continually at work through his Spirit. The God of the Bible can only be known by taking him " at his word "; in other words, through commitment. Faith means responding to his mighty deeds by commitment. " If you continue in my word, . . . you will know the truth, and the truth will make you free." (John 8:31-32.) There is no other way to " knowledge " than the way of faith and obedience. The Holy Spirit is the divine witness who seals in the heart the words of God's earthly witnesses, so that, again and again throughout the centuries, these words become the "Word of God" to the listening and praying church and shape its life as well as its faith.

The church has to rediscover again and again its vocation, its *corporate vocation* as the witnessing community taken out of the world, *set apart* for God, but set apart in order to be again *sent* to the world. "Set apart" — "sent to." The tension between these two terms has constantly to be kept in mind if we are to grasp the vocation of God's People all through history. A superficial reading of the Bible might lead us to think that the Old Testament is centered entirely on the destiny of Israel. The foreign nations are dealt with only in so far as they interfere with the life of Israel or are used by God in the fulfillment of his purpose for his chosen People. Furthermore, the apostolic church seems mainly concerned with the upbuilding of the community as over against the "world."

All this is true, yet we misinterpret the Biblical message if we do not see the *instrumental* function of God's People; separation and mission are the two aspects of the call to be a witnessing community. The goal is a world reconciled with God. In the very first chapters of the Bible, God's concern for the world is revealed not only in his creative act but in his will to maintain life, in his renewed covenant with mankind. Abraham's call is to be a blessing for "all the families of the earth." Israel's greatest prophets proclaim that God is not only Lord of Israel but Lord of history. Jesus proclaims God's universal Kingship, and for him salvation means entering the Kingdom, being taken into the great fellowship of God's realm. The Bible ends with a vision of the City of God into which all nations bring glory and honor. God's People are both the ambassadors and the token, the heralds and the visible sign, of his redeeming purpose.

Two temptations constantly threaten the witnessing community. One is to consider the separate life as an end in itself. This produces a ghetto religion, the self-righteousness of the Pharisee, the exclusiveness of the " saved." The other is to succumb to a slow process of assimilation by which God's People lose their identity and adopt the way of life of the pagan or secular civilization which surrounds them. Israel conquers Canaan, but the Baals conquer Israel; the church conquers the Roman Empire but becomes a secularized church, salt that has lost its taste. Therefore, God is shown relentlessly pruning his vine, cutting away the dead branches, in order to save the stem without which his whole redeeming purpose would be thwarted. The Old Testament presents us with a series of such prunings. Election means the selection of a given man, tribe, people; but these are never set apart because of their special merit or for their own sake: they are instruments of God's ongoing purpose — the salvation of the world. We see God's People reduced to a "remnant," until "the times are fulfilled," and the remnant gives birth to the One who could say of himself that the Ruler of this world had no power over him.

Christ's self-offering, his victory over sin and death, gives birth to a new body, the Church — born "not of the flesh but of the Spirit," born from above. This enables our Lord to say that those who belong to him are " in " but not " of " the world. As his Father has sent him into the world, so does he send his disciples into the world: yet as long as they are " in the flesh," the world is also in them. Therefore the church and its members will suffer the same tensions as God's People of old, and the same temptations: the temptation to withdraw from the world in order to save their souls; the temptation to adapt to the world by accepting its standards and goals — possibly in the sincere desire to become " all things to all men."

Thus we have continually to ask ourselves which master we serve, not in principle only, but in the concrete facts of daily life. Are we really and truly the kind of community that will startle the world by the quality of its relationships, so that the world may believe in Him who sent us? Are we the city on the hill to which a distraught world will turn for guidance and help, as a weary traveler turns to the light? Are we " in the world " as Christ was, sharing its sufferings, carrying its burdens? Are we, on the other hand, " not of the world," separate from the world as Christ wants us to be: a redeemed community which lives by grace in a world that believes in works, power, and success? Are our standards Christ's or the world's?

The Bible faces us with these questions. These are the questions with which Israel had to wrestle as God's covenanted People, the questions with which the church can never cease to wrestle to the end of time. What did it mean to be God's People in 800 B.C.? What does it mean to be the church in A.D. 1958? Let us be questioned anew by the living God who speaks through the Bible, whose Word is a two-edged sword.

A few words may be needed here as to the way in which the author of this book approaches the Biblical message. We are quite aware of the many literary problems the Bible poses. There are, particularly in the early books of the Old Testament, many layers of tradition, still partly recognizable, which by a long process have been fused into one continuous story. There was a long period of oral tradition before these books were put into writing. How far are they history, how far saga? For our modern mind there is a tendency to consider history as true and saga as invention, but this is a misconception of the way in which the human mind works. Saga is to chronicle what poetry is to prose. It reveals the very soul of a people. All our attempts to disentangle saga and history are based on more or less unstable hypotheses, and it is found today, thanks to more archaeological knowledge, that the historical background of the patriarchal stories, for instance, is much more accurate than scholars tended to admit fifty years ago. We shall not attempt here, therefore, to disentangle saga and history: the Bible as it now stands is meant to convey a definite message, and it is this message that

matters. It tells about the deeds of God, about God's divine
purpose unfolding itself in history.

The Old Testament is an unfinished story: it looks forward
to the Messiah to come, to God's ultimate victory. As Christians,
we read the whole story in the light of its fulfillment in Christ.
It is said of the risen Christ that he opened the minds of his
disciples and " interpreted to them in all the scriptures the things
concerning himself " (Luke 24:27; see also vs. 32, 44–45). The
apostolic church is unanimous in seeing in the coming, death,
and elevation of Jesus Christ the fulfillment of Old Testament
prophecy. But this prophecy is seen in both word and deed. The
saving acts of God in the Old Testament are prophetic: they
point to the greater reality yet to come. This is what Paul means
when he says that to the Jews the Old Testament message is still
" veiled " and that in Christ " the veil is removed " (see II Cor.
3:12–18).

The fathers of the church and the sixteenth-century Reformers shared this conviction that Jesus Christ is the true interpreter
of the Scriptures and that the Old Testament should be read in
that light. This certainly does not mean that we should ignore
the historical setting of a given event. God speaks and acts in
history; he always speaks concretely. But it does mean that
there is a continuity of God's purpose manifesting itself all
through the discontinuities of human history. This is the divine
history within history. That it was given to prophets and apostles to discern this divine operation of God within history and
to bear witness to his saving grace is the very essence of revelation. For " no one comprehends the thoughts of God except the
Spirit of God " (I Cor. 2:11).

At the same time, the instruments of revelation are human.
Commenting on Moses' complaint that he was " slow of speech "
(Ex. 4:10), Buber writes: " The tragedy of Moses becomes the
tragedy inherent in revelation. It is laid upon the stammering
to bring the voice of heaven to earth." When man uses human

language to describe his encounter with the reality of God, what can he do but stammer? This is the human side of the Bible. Yet through this stammering, God speaks and acts. This is the divine side. One could speak of the two natures of the Book as one speaks of the two natures of Christ: God accepts the limitations of human nature in order to speak to our conditions *from within*. And the two natures are inseparable. We are not able to draw a clear line in the Bible and to say, " This is of God," and " This is of man." We have to listen to the Bible as a whole, remembering always that its center, beginning, and end is Christ. We have to let the Spirit do his work as divine witness, sealing the written word in our hearts as a word from God for us today. As we do this, the message steadily grows, and we read the Bible with an ever deeper sense of wonder and awe. Of its most obscure parts, we may be able to say someday, " Surely the Lord is in this place; and I did not know it " (Gen. 28:16).

CHAPTER I

Broken Relationships

"Let us make a name for ourselves." (Gen. 11:4.)

We live in a world of broken relationships. This is a hard fact of daily life. The struggle for power and the need for self-assertion make for secret or open conflict in home and factory, in economics and politics. Our world stands under the sign of suffering and strife, of decay and death. Why all this? The early chapters of Genesis offer part of the answer. We say " part of the answer " because the full, victorious answer will be given by the New Testament.

Man in God's Image
   Genesis is the book of the beginnings. It tells about God's will to create a harmonious world: " And God saw everything that he had made, and behold, it was very good." (Gen. 1:31.) It tells about man's unique vocation as a steward of God's creation. God speaks to man and calls him to free and joyful service. He thus creates a unique I–Thou relationship, a relationship that implies trust, love, and obedience. " ' Let us make man in our image, after our likeness; and let them have dominion over the fish of the sea, and over the birds of the air, and over the cattle, and over all the earth, and over every creeping thing that creeps upon the earth.' So God created man in his own image, in the image of God he created him; male and female he created them." (Gen. 1:26–27.)

What is meant when it is said that God made man in his image and likeness? In contrast with his creation of the animal world, God makes of man and woman his responsible partners. He establishes an I–Thou relationship. He " speaks " to them; he entrusts them with a stewardship. Probably the aim of the writer was to underline the uniqueness of this relationship. The remark in Gen. 9:6 — " Whoever sheds the blood of man, by man shall his blood be shed; for God made man in his own image " — indicates that even fallen man bears this unique mark of his relation to God.

What is the force of the " us " of Gen. 1:26? Is it a " plural of majesty," as some would hold? Or is it, as others contend, a literary slip due to the polytheistic stories from which the theme was borrowed (an unthinkable mistake on the part of the priestly circles who preserved this document for us!) ? Whatever the intention of the writer, the faith of the Christian will read " beyond " what is written. The Christian reader will be struck by the fact that it is the man-woman community which is to reflect God. God does not create man in isolation. He creates him as a community, as man and woman. The Trinitarian God is a fellowship of love and can only be reflected on the human plane in a living relationship. Only a human " we " can reflect something of the divine " us."

The ultimate meaning of Gen. 1:26–27 can be grasped only when in Christ the " veil " is lifted and God's purpose is fully revealed. " He is the image of the invisible God, the first-born of all creation; for in him all things were created." (Col. 1:15–16.) Jesus Christ is true Man, the pre-existent Son of Man in whom God's nature is reflected, through whom mankind will attain its ultimate goal. This is the Christian answer to the riddle of Gen. 1:26. What we must grasp now, however, is that from the very beginning God created community. The man-woman relationship is the first nucleus of that wider community which is to be called into being. The I–Thou relationship between God and man is to be reflected in the I–Thou relationship of man and woman. This finds an even more explicit and beautiful expression in the story told in the second chapter of Genesis when man welcomes woman with a cry of acknowledgment and joy as flesh of his flesh and bone of his bones. " And they become one flesh. And the man and his wife were both naked, and were not ashamed." (Gen. 2:24–25.) The Paradise condition is one of transparence. God sees through his creatures and they see through each other: love is unstained by pride and self-defense.

God's Image Marred

The third chapter of Genesis tells, in story form, of a threefold break in relationship: between God and the human couple, between man and wife, between man and the world that surrounds him. The essential theological truth revealed in this chapter is that all the tensions and disruptions of mankind go back to a fundamental disruption produced by the *will to autonomy* of the creature as over against the Creator. " You will be like God." (Gen. 3:5.) In snatching at equality with God, in wanting to be their own masters and to stand in their own right, woman and man destroy the childlike trust that makes them open to God's love and purpose and to one another. Lust for power has entered the world and will henceforth be at the root of all antagonism between sexes, between brothers, between groups, nations, and races. Having lost our at-one-ness with God, we become like self-centered tops, turning round and round upon ourselves. We do this as individuals; we do it collectively on a world scale.

The startling insight of the Genesis story is further shown in the fact that as soon as their eyes are " opened " man and woman hide from one another and hide from the presence of God. The transparence is lost. Our instinct is to hide because being seen as we are would be unbearable. We do not hide from one another only, but from ourselves. We acquire the gift of covering our guilt from our own eyes: " *She* gave me fruit of the tree, and I ate." (Gen. 3:12.) The tragedy of the sexes is described in one sentence: " Your desire shall be for your husband, and he shall rule over you." (Gen. 3:16.) The joyful encounter is now shadowed by the will to dominate. Man's authority will be corrupted by his lust for power. Woman will try to overcome him by more subtle means. The two sexes at the same time attract and antagonize each other.

Another break of relationship appears in the story: ceasing to be God's steward, man will be in constant tension and strife with the world he was meant to tend and subdue. His will-to-power expresses itself in ruthless exploitation. Joyful work becomes hard labor.

A story like Gen., ch. 3, raises many questions in our minds. The Bible does not attempt to explain the origin of evil. It simply states the fact: we do live in a world the harmony of which is disrupted by evil. Yet it is important to note, as over against similar myths in pagan religions, that the serpent, which in the story symbolizes the power of evil, is a *creature,* not an eternal principle as found, for instance, in Persian dualism. From beginning to end the Bible affirms God's exclusive sovereignty. Again, it is difficult for us to situate the Fall in history. Suffering and death have existed in the animal world long before man appeared on this planet; we cannot imagine the world we know as " good ": our experience is of a " paradise lost." Adam personifies natural man in his standing revolt against God. Whenever the initial break took place, his story is our story. " The first man was from the earth, a man of dust [" Adam " means " man," and the word is derived from " earth " (*adama*)]; the second man is from heaven." (I Cor. 15:47.) We belong by nature to this world of strife and will-to-power so accurately described in Gen., ch. 3; we are a part of this mankind which mistook autonomy for liberty and found enslavement;

a mankind that has the fearful possibility — alone among all earthly creatures — of saying no to God, and bearing the consequences. Why did this have to happen? The cruel enigma of a world gone astray can be solved only when we look at Jesus Christ, the image of the invisible God in whom the destiny of man takes on its real and ultimate meaning, in whom freedom is revealed as being found in the response of love to love, in the surrender of our wills to God's.

The whole story of God's redeeming purpose in history is one of restored unity. Its background is the state of broken relationships described in the story of Gen., ch. 3. Paul certainly had this chapter in mind when he described Christ as not snatching at equality with God — although Christ was in the form of God, yet he took the form of a servant. Natural man's way pushes upward; God's way is the downward way of merciful love — voluntary identification with the downtrodden and lost. In the light of the cross we see ourselves as we are, and if by the grace of God we stop " hiding," we learn the reality of forgiveness. Then and then only can we dare to be " seen through " and begin to recover our transparence, to see ourselves as we are, and to accept one another. To study the Bible is to study the long path from false to true liberty, from false autonomy to true manhood as revealed and shown in Christ, from self-centeredness to community.

Community Destroyed

Chapters 4 to 11 of Genesis show the consequences of the broken relationship between man and his Maker. A divisive force is now at work which throws brother against brother, tribe against tribe. Every new conquest of mankind becomes a two-edged sword, breeding disaster as well as advance. The story of the first murder is significant. Whether there lies behind it the old rivalry between the shepherd and the laborer who tills the land remains an open question. The motive given for the

murder is Cain's resentment when Abel's offering is acceptable
to God and his own is not. Jesus recognizes in Abel the fore-
runner and " type " of the servants of God who throughout history have been slaughtered because their existence stood as a
judgment upon the hard hearts of those who rejected God and
neighbor. (See Matt. 23:35.) What is true of Abel and the
prophets is true of Jesus himself: his presence will very quickly
become unbearable to Pharisees and Sadducees because if he is
right, all their piety, all their endeavors, are reduced to nought.

In what a lively way the story goes: Cain's countenance falls;
the Lord warns him that sin is " couching at the door " (Gen.
4:7)! Hatred bears murder. Yet God does not completely forsake the murderer. Cain goes out of the presence of God, but
God " marks " him. Still he remains in God's keeping. Cain
loses sight of God. God does not lose sight of Cain. He does not
abandon his lost world to itself.

The discovery of iron meant as great a revolution in the history of primitive mankind as nuclear fission has brought in our
day. The descendants of Cain are said to be the first to forge instruments of bronze and iron; this means a great step forward
toward civilization. But how significant again is Lamech's cry:

> " I have slain a man for wounding me,
>   a young man for striking me.
> If Cain is avenged sevenfold,
>   truly Lamech seventy-sevenfold "!
>   (Gen. 4:23-24.)

Science and technology in a sinful world will always be powers
for destruction as well as advancement. Here the first achievement of technology was a weapon of destruction, the sword. In
our day, the first great achievement of the newly acquired
knowledge was the atomic bomb.

The Cainites are said to have built the first city, invented the
first effective weapon and the first instruments of music. How

strikingly the Bible describes here the ambivalent character of culture when detached from God! Man is not deprived of his natural gifts; he can create beauty. But always the will-to-power poisons his most promising achievements. In 1945, I heard a well-known professor say confidently to his students, "Science has now come to the point where man is master of things; soon he will be master of his own destiny." A week later the first bomb fell on Hiroshima.

Masters of our own destiny . . . !

No glorious invention is attributed to the children of Shem. It is simply said of some of them that they " walked with God " (Gen. 5:24). This too may have a symbolic meaning: the Hebrews as " children of Shem " have contributed little to the general culture of the ancient world. Nothing will single them out except one thing: their call to " walk with God." It is God's strange way to choose for his work a people who have really, humanly speaking, nothing to boast about.

A New Covenant

The tradition of a great destructive flood is common to a number of ancient Eastern peoples. The Biblical account is again unique by the theological significance given to the event: it faces us with God's judgment and God's grace, with the great principle of election — but election in view of a mission. Noah and his family are set apart, saved from universal destruction to be the stem from which a new mankind will grow; not only a new mankind but a new *world:* every species is represented in the ark. The church will see a symbol of its own destiny in this tiny vessel tossed on the waves, carrying the promises of life, the future of the world. This family " saved through water," by faith, this tiny community, is a sign and token of God's faithfulness. It was interpreted by the early church as a symbol of baptism, understood as a dying and rising again (I Peter 3:18–22). But what about those who were destroyed?

Will there be an opportunity for them to meet Christ and accept salvation? The First Letter of Peter suggests an affirmative answer to this question (I Peter 3:19–20). The election of Noah is related to God's plan of salvation for the whole world and does not imply any concepts of personal predestination to eternal life or death. Already in this early story we have an illustration of the instrumental function of God's chosen people.

The God of the Bible is a living God, a dynamic God. To convey this, the writers do not hesitate to use anthropomorphic language — the only language we possess to describe the movements of the heart. God pledges himself never again to proceed by such radical destruction: " I will never again curse the ground because of man, for the imagination of man's heart is evil from his youth; neither will I ever again destroy every living creature as I have done. While the earth remains, seedtime and harvest, cold and heat, summer and winter, day and night, shall not cease." (Gen. 8:21–22.) God has no illusion left as to the heart of men; the maintenance of the world is on his part an act of sheer mercy. This conviction that the very continuance of life, the rhythm of seasons, of nights and days, is maintained only by God's grace, runs through the whole Bible; it fills the psalmist with thankfulness and awe. Jesus will say that not a sparrow is forgotten in the sight of God. God's first covenant is " with every living creature " (Gen. 9:10), and it is only in this wider context that the specific covenant with " a peculiar people " can be understood. It is an " everlasting " covenant between God and all flesh and, on God's part, an unconditional one.

To Noah and his sons, a special blessing is given. God not only restores them to a definite relation with him; he also reestablishes a certain relation between them and the animal world — not the paradisaic relationship, but one conditioned by sin: " The fear of you and the dread of you shall be upon every beast of the earth. . . . Every moving thing that lives shall be food for you; and as I gave you the green plants, I give you everything." (Gen. 9:2-3.) The ancient notion that the soul (the psychic life) is in the blood leads, however, to the command never to eat animal blood, a commandment deeply engraved in the Jewish consciousness to this day (Gen. 9:4; see also on this point Acts 15:20). The shedding of human blood will be avenged: respect for human life is enjoined here as the basic rule of any communal existence. Why should we respect life? Because "God made man in his own image" (Gen. 9:6). In this long story of broken relationships God maintains his sovereign right over the human soul; to destroy life is to take away what belongs to Another. The mirror in which God's will and love were to be reflected is now broken; it presents a distorted image; but the mark is still there, and God's claim is inalienable. The murderer is responsible to God for every drop of shed blood — without exception of person or race. Here we have a basic law of life, binding for all men (see Gen. 9:5-6).

The story of Noah's drunkenness illustrates another tradition deeply engraved in the unwritten code of the ancient East, namely, the respect of the father. The two sons who cover their father's sin are blessed. The story has evidently also an etiological significance: it tends to justify the domination of the children of Shem over the children of Ham — of Israel over Canaan. It is rather tragic that this story should have been misused in modern times to justify the domination of the white race (Japheth) over the Negro race (Cush), and even to justify slavery!

A Name for Themselves

In the eleventh chapter of Genesis, the story of the Tower of Babel illustrates the *collective lust for power*. In the second millennium B.C., Babylon was at a high point of glory. The memory of this city, of its towering temples, of its rise and downfall, is probably the concrete fact that left its mark on sur-

rounding nations. But the story has a wider significance: to
" make a name for [themselves] " is the standing temptation of
all great powers. This attempt to dominate the world ends in
" confusion." (The Hebrew writer plays here on the Hebrew
word " *balal*," confusion). Language is a means of communication. The multiplicity of languages means a break in communication. This is seen as God's curse on an artificial unity built
from beneath, built on lust and pride. The Bible teaches us
again and again the vanity of empires resting on such foundations: the vertigo of earthly power leads to doom. We shall
come back at a later stage to the prophets' judgment on Tyre,
the queen of the seas, on Egypt, Nineveh, and Babylon (the
second Babylonian Empire). The fundamental sin is always the
same: " You have said, ' I am a god.' " (Ezek. 28:2.) The rise
and fall of Tyre is seen as a parable of the myth of Creation: it
was " the signet of perfection, full of wisdom and perfect in
beauty," until " in the abundance of . . . [its] trade" it was
" filled with violence " — and fell (Ezek. 28:12, 16)!

The breakdown of empires is thus seen as having the same
source as the original Fall. The claim to be like a god, free from
all boundaries of good and evil, leads ultimately to sheer destruction.

At the end of these early chapters of Genesis, we are thus
faced with a tragic picture of destruction: it starts with the basic
community — the couple; it extends to the family, to the tribe,
to the world of nations. This is the background against which
the story of the chosen People has to be seen. God has not abandoned mankind to its fate. The long story that follows is one
of slow and patient preparation, until the time comes for the
Second Adam to lift the curse of sin and death and for the Spirit
of Pentecost to create a unity from above — the divine counterpart to all Towers of Babel.

CHAPTER **II**

A New Beginning

" I will bless you, and make your name great, so that you will be a blessing." (Gen. 12:2.)

We have seen how Genesis, the book of "beginnings," started with the creation of the world and the creation of man. We have seen that the covenant with Noah meant another new beginning, God's pact of enduring patience with a fallen mankind. Chapter 12 of Genesis, however, marks an even more decisive new beginning: the calling into being of a People, the People of God.

A Wandering Aramean

We know today that in the third millennium before Christ great civilizations had developed. But God chose for his purpose an unknown man, a " wandering Aramean "; He built up a tribe to claim as *his* tribe, among all peoples of the earth. Israel has kept a strikingly clear memory of these humble beginnings. When the Israelite approaches the altar and presents his gift to the priest, he recites a confession of faith opening with words that present-day scholars tend to look upon as Israel's most ancient confession of faith: "A wandering Aramean was my father. . . ." (Deut. 26:5.)

In the story of the Shechem covenant, Joshua is reported to have said: " Thus says the Lord, the God of Israel, ' Your fathers lived of old beyond the Euphrates, Terah, the father of Abra-

ham and of Nahor; and they served other gods. Then I took
your father Abraham from beyond the River and led him
through all the land of Canaan, and made his offspring many.' "
(Josh. 24:2–3.) " Hebrew national tradition," writes Professor
Albright, "excels all others in its clear picture of tribal and
family life. In Egypt and Babylonia, in Assyria and Phoenicia,
in Greece and Rome, we look in vain for anything comparable."
(" The Biblical Period," *The Jews: Their History, Culture, and
Religion,* ed. by L. Finkelstein. Harper & Brothers, 1949.)

Scholars have for a long time expressed skepticism as to the
historical background of the patriarchal cycle of stories. This
skepticism has been shaken in the last decades: recent archaeological discoveries have shown the accuracy of Biblical data as to
times, places, and names. We know, for instance, that the Babylonian city of Ur-Kasdim was at the height of prosperity around
2000 B.C. and was destroyed in 1960 B.C. We know that there was
at the time a migration of Amorites toward Mesopotamia,
Amorite being a general name for Semites coming from the
northwest (later the term Amorite designates one specific tribe).
Names such as Abram, Jacob, Laban, Zebulun, Benjamin are to
be found among the Amorites of that period. (How far the
names mentioned were those of tribes rather than people is
difficult to ascertain. In the ongoing tradition the ancestor tends
to become a personification of the tribe.) We know of Haran
as a city which prospered in the nineteenth and eighteenth centuries B.C.

Most peoples have traditions put in the form of stories or
sagas, which are transmitted from generation to generation and
express the deepest realities of their soul. Such stories generally
tend to glorify the ancestor; he embodies the virtues for which
a given people stand, or claim to stand. The striking and unique
feature of Israel's traditions about the ancestors of the tribe is
that they do not attempt to make heroes of those about whom
they tell. The main actor in the story is God. Abraham's venture

of faith describes in a dramatic way the mission to which Israel knows itself to be committed: to him was the promise given by which they live; this wandering Aramean faces the temptations and tests that the wandering tribes will have to go through before reaching the Holy Land. But, through it all, it is God who calls, who leads, who delivers. And the very weaknesses of Israel are reflected in the ancestor's thrift, doubts, or bargainings.

Call and Promise

The call of God comes first of all to Abram as a call to " go out "! " He went out, not knowing where he was to go." (Heb. 11:8; see also Gen. 12:1.) To make a new beginning, God takes this man out of his surroundings: he has to leave his father's house, the place where he was settled; he has to leave behind everything that ties him to the past, and, most of all, he has to leave his gods. What these gods were, we are not told. To understand the nature of the break implied in these few and sober words, we must remember the tribal system in which religious, social, and cultural life is so closely knit that to be cut off from the tribe is to lose one's identity, is to be like a branch severed from its stem. Only if we see this, can the full scope of God's promise be understood: " I will make of you a great nation, . . . in you all the families of the earth will be blessed." (Gen. 12:2–3, margin.) Community destroyed and community rebuilt!

God's blessing is conceived as a real communication of power and life. God's blessing is shown in the bearing of children, in abundant flocks or crops. But these words are spoken to a childless couple. God's promise is not supported by facts. Abram is to take God at his word and to risk his all on this word. " So Abram went." This is faith. By this simple act of obedience, Abram becomes the father of all believers. Faith as revealed in the Bible is staking our whole lives on God's word, on his call and commandment. Jesus' claim will be no less absolute than this first call to break all former ties and " go out." " No one

who puts his hand to the plow and looks back is fit for the kingdom of God." (Luke 9:62.) He who thus goes out will "be a
blessing." The severance of natural ties can only be a means for
wider service. A new tribe, the Tribe of God, is to be born.

How strange are God's ways! Babylon has disappeared, except as an object of archaeological research. Its name was great
for a while — and then forgotten. But the Aramean nomad is
claimed as an ancestor by the Jews, the Christians, and even the
Moslems — whether an ancestor according to the flesh or according to the spirit. "Look toward heaven, and number the
stars, if you are able to number them. . . . So shall your descendants be." (Gen. 15:5.) God's promise holds good.

"And he believed the Lord; and he reckoned it to him as
righteousness." (Gen. 15:6.) Righteousness, if we go back to
the Hebrew root of the word, is a concept of relationship, of
straight relationship. God's righteousness is manifested in his
faithfulness to the covenant. A man is considered "righteous"
by God if he responds to the relationship that God in his mercy
has established with him; and this implies trust and obedience
on man's side. To believe is to take God at his word, to stake
one's whole life and hope on him alone. This is what the childless Abram does when faced with the unbelievable promise of
an innumerable posterity. Why this frequent insistence in the
patriarchal stories on the barrenness of women? The son of the
promise is a gift of God's grace, and must be received as such.
Therefore, the faith of the mother is put to the test: she has to
wait for God's hour.

God's Covenant with His People

Chapter 15 of Genesis tells, in a very ancient form, of God's
covenant with Abram. The ritual described here must have
been very well known in Israel; it was followed in Jeremiah's
time (Jer. 34:18). When two parties concluded a solemn pact,
their representatives passed between animals that had been cut

in two, signifying by this act that they expected to be treated in the same way if they should ever break the covenant. The Genesis story has a dramatic touch. Abram has made all things ready as ordered. It is evening. A deep sleep falls on him. " And lo, a dread and great darkness fell upon him." (Gen. 15:12.) In this darkness Abram sees a flaming torch pass between the parted animals. What does this mean? The nearness of God, the pledge that is going to bind a weak man to the Holy God, always fills the elect with awe. This " dread " is mentioned several times in the Old Testament; it overtakes a man when God reveals himself to him and charges him with a mission to fulfill. Jacob on his way to the Promised Land, Moses on his way to Egypt, are thus mysteriously " attacked " by God. Awe is the normal feeling of a sinful creature set apart to serve the Holy One. The flame passing between the animals means that God takes upon himself the full weight of the covenant. Abram is not requested to pass between them. Not only the initiation but the fulfillment of the covenant lies in God's hand.

When reading this mysterious story, a Christian cannot but remember all the broken covenants of which the Bible tells; indeed, if God's faithfulness were dependent on ours, we would be lost. The full answer posed by the problem of man's unfaithfulness is not seen until God, in Christ, takes upon himself the sin of the defaulting partner, and builds the new covenant at the price of vicarious suffering and death. Only on this basis could an everlasting covenant be built. The writer of Gen., ch. 15, did not know the end of the story. But he knew that the only hope for Abram, as for us, lay in God's faithfulness.

Chapter 17 of Genesis gives us a different account of God's covenant with Abram: it lacks the freshness of the preceding story, although the essential elements — the promise, the call — are the same. We have to do here with the so-called priestly document; it is recognizable even in translation by its heavier and more solemn style, its interest in genealogies and in the origins of cultic institutions. (We cannot in this brief study enter into the literary problems of the Pentateuch. We refer the reader to a study such as "The Growth of the Hexateuch," by C. A. Simpson, in the first volume of *The Interpreter's Bible*. Abingdon Press, 1952.) Here God orders the circumcision of all males as the sign of the covenant. It should be noted at once that no social exclusiveness is implicit in this rite: the foreigner living in the tribe should be submitted to it. It is on this solemn occasion that God changes Abram's name to Abraham — " exalted father," and Sarai's to Sarah — " my princess." He renews his promise that Sarah will have a son, and Abraham " fell on his face and laughed " (Gen. 17:17). His total skepticism is expressed in his cry: " Oh that Ishmael might live in thy sight! " (Gen. 17:18.) His hope does not lie in God's promise, but in the son that nature has provided for him.

Again, how much more vivid are the two Hagar-Ishmael stories that we find in chs. 16 and 21! We are faced with the ancient tribal custom that allowed the childless woman to give her maid to her husband as a concubine and then to adopt the child. But soon Sarai's heart is torn by hatred and jealousy. Abram does nothing to protect Hagar, and she runs away. But the angel of the Lord stops her flight and sends her back to her mistress. The commandment is followed by a promise that her descendants will be great. More dramatic even is the second story, in ch. 21, where we see mother and child driven into the desert. " And God heard the voice of the lad. . . . And God was with the lad." (Gen. 21:17, 20.)

In both stories — the aim of which may be partly to explain the origin of the Ishmaelites — we see that God's care is never understood as limited to those within the covenant. His mercy follows the forsaken woman and her boy into the wilderness and quenches their thirst. For them too there is a promise of life.

How shall we interpret the story, to be found in different

form twice in the life of Abram and once in that of Isaac, of the patriarch presenting his wife as his sister? (See Gen. 12:10–20; chs. 20; 26.) There may be behind such stories a very human glorification of the beauty of the women ancestors of the tribe! To us, Abram and Isaac appear as shocking cowards, selling their wives for safety's sake; we find it difficult to understand the spirit of these times. But what these stories are meant to convey to us is God's faithfulness to his promise: he keeps Abram and Sarai from destruction in spite of themselves; he watches over his own and no one is allowed to touch them. To harm them is to offend God.

Genesis, ch. 18, is a beautiful illustration of hospitality as conceived in patriarchal times and as it still can be found among nomads. The weary traveler is welcomed and honored, his sore feet are washed, he is asked to accept " a morsel of bread," while both the lord of the house and the housewife get busy preparing a plenteous meal; a calf is killed, cakes " of fine meal " are prepared. The quality of the guests is soon revealed by a promise which leaves Sarah laughing behind the tent door. (Rembrandt has painted a famous picture of the guests and of Sarah laughing behind their backs.) The Lord reads her heart and she immediately denies that she has laughed. In welcoming the unknown visitors, Abraham has welcomed the Lord himself. (The Greek Orthodox Church has Christianized this by seeing in the three men an epiphany of the Trinity. One of the most beautiful icons of the Russian Church represents the Trinity in the form of the three mysterious guests, linked to one another as in a graceful circular movement.)

But there is a second phase in the story: the Lord takes Abraham into his confidence and tells him about the impending judgment on Sodom and Gomorrah. Abraham pleads, "Wilt thou indeed destroy the righteous with the wicked? " (Gen. 18:23.) A strange dialogue follows, where man seems to stand for righteousness and mercy, compelling God to ever-growing concessions. The problem raised here is whether the presence of five just men can save the community. God will not spare the wicked cities, but he will save Lot. Sodom and Gomorrah will remain in Israel's tradition the very symbols of corruption. How stern, against such a background, sound the words of Jesus about those who reject him: "Truly, I say to you, it shall be more tolerable on the day of judgment for the land of Sodom and Gomorrah than for that town." (Matt. 10:15.) There are for men and groups hours when the choice is one of life and death.

Faith Tested

Chapter 22 of Genesis is the most poignant story of the Old Testament. It is presented to us as the supreme test of Abraham's faith. "'Take your son, your only son Isaac, whom you love, and go to the land of Moriah, and offer him there as a burnt offering upon one of the mountains of which I shall tell you.' So Abraham rose early in the morning." (Gen. 22:2-3.) Nothing is said of the anxiety of this father's heart. He does not discuss God's orders. He goes.

Christians who read this story today are often puzzled and shocked. A man who would believe that God orders him to kill his child would be considered insane today. We must remember the background of the story, the current practice of child-offering in Canaan. At the same time, we miss its significance if we try to escape the problem by saying that Abraham only imagined that God required this of him while He, of course, made no such request. The story means that the test was intended and terribly real. The fathers of the church and the Reformers felt acutely its paradoxical character. Says Saint Chrysostom: "God contradicts God, faith contradicts faith. The commandment contradicts the promise." And Luther writes: "God openly contradicts himself. Human reason is shaken and only faith can make the jump and lean on God's sole promise. . . .

Abraham has understood the article of faith which declares the resurrection of the dead."

The great paradox of the story certainly lies in the fact that God seems to destroy his own work in destroying the child on whom all his promises rest. Shall we say with Luther that Abraham believed the resurrection of the dead? Or shall we say that he had to go through the black night of obedience without understanding? How he has grown since the time when he tried to make God's promises come true by human means! These three days of solitary walking to the place of sacrifice were perhaps in Jesus' mind when he said, " I must go on my way today and tomorrow and the day following," speaking of his last journey to Jerusalem (Luke 13:33). So God delivers Isaac in the last moment. But he will not spare his own son!

Abraham remains throughout the ages the veritable type of the believer not only because he receives everything from the hand of God, but because he is ready at any time to give it back to God. In the life of Christians there are moments when we walk in darkness, and must give up our most beloved ones, our most cherished hopes. We have to give God a blank check of faith and obedience. Then only can we understand something of the agony of " our father in the faith."

There is a page in the cycle of the Abraham stories that we have not mentioned. It stands apart in some ways: the story of the war in which Abraham takes part to save his nephew, Lot. Tribal faithfulness remains, even though Lot has been selfish in choosing the land he thought to be the best. In his relation to his nephew, Abraham is always the greater, the more self-sacrificing one. He shows his character again in refusing his share of the spoils. The most important episode is that of Melchizedek (king of righteousness), king and priest of Salem (" Salem " means " peace " and probably designates the future of Jerusalem), who blesses Abraham in the name of the " Most High." The Letter to the Hebrews later sees in this mysterious figure of Melchizedek a prefiguration of Christ.

We have dealt at length with Abraham, both because he is the father of the "new tribe" to be, and because he holds a unique place in the New Testament. To him is made the great promise which is to be fulfilled ultimately in Christ; he starts in faith the pilgrimage toward the Holy Land, the land that is itself only a token of the Kingdom to come. "For he looked forward to the city which has foundations, whose builder and maker is God." (Heb. 11:10.)

The Mystery of Election

We shall turn now for a brief moment to the other "fathers." The marriage of Isaac illustrates the concern to maintain the integrity of the tribe. It also shows the freedom and dignity that women enjoyed in patriarchal times: Rebekah's consent to the marriage is asked. And the story ends with the simple statement that "Isaac brought her into the tent, and took Rebekah, and she became his wife; and he loved her" (Gen. 24:67).

The Jacob cycle of stories has more far-reaching significance. We are faced with what seems to be the arbitrariness of election. Why has the Lord "loved Jacob" and "hated Esau"? (See Mal. 1:1-5 and Rom. 9:13.) Is not the hatred of two tribes, Israel and Edom, charged against God? And are not human passions rather than God's choice at the root of the matter? Paul does not think so; neither does the ancient writer of the story. Election means a free choice of God which precedes any volition of man. The destiny of the twins is announced before they have left their mother's womb. This does not preclude human responsibility. We are faced here with a paradox which runs all through the Bible: God works out his purpose in history; he calls, he rejects, he guides. But this never excludes human responsibility; for this responsibility is part of God's plan. Human logic is baffled. Yet our spiritual experience confirms that both affirmations must be kept in a living tension: God's election and our freedom. We are saved by grace — yet responsible beings. Our " amen " to God is a free " yes."

The partiality of the father for Esau, of the mother for Jacob, are parts of the tragedy. But Esau, when he sells his birthright for a bowl of lentil pottage, commits the greatest sin conceivable in those times: he renounces the "blessing" which the father gave to the eldest son. In this case it means not only giving up the father's heritage, but giving up his place in the line of the promise.

Jacob is not described in favorable terms: he is a liar, unscrupulous, ruthless. But he cares for the "blessing." He is marked by God as the heir of the promise. He will be chastened for his sins and he will know a long exile, but God will be with him. There are two significant encounters with the living God in Jacob's life. The first was on his flight to Haran, when he sees " a ladder set up on the earth, and the top of it reached to heaven; and behold, the angels of God were ascending and descending on it! . . . Then Jacob awoke from his sleep and said, ' Surely the Lord is in this place; and I did not know it.' " (Gen. 28:12, 16.) Here again we see God's self-revelation filling a man with wonder and awe. The second encounter takes place on Jacob's return, after many long years. His thrift has made him rich, but his heart is filled with anxiety. And in the night " a man " wrestles with him. Jacob prays: " I will not let you go, unless you bless me." (Gen. 32:26.) This mysterious struggle leaves him lame; but he has conquered: " Your name shall no more be called Jacob, but Israel, for you have striven with God and with men, and have prevailed." (Gen. 32:28.)

This is election: God of his own free choice laying his hand on an unworthy man and using him as an instrument of his saving purpose, training him and chastening him. The man can kick against the spurs, he may disobey and betray. But God does not let him go until the purpose is fulfilled.

The destiny of Jacob is the destiny of Israel. The chosen People will have to go the path of exile. Their history will be a long striving with God and with men. As a people they will be defeated again and again, and only God's mercy will save them from destruction. God will preserve a " remnant " and the "true Israel" will be born: Jesus Christ. He is the only one of whom it can be fully said that he has " striven with God and with men, and . . . prevailed." He will conquer by going through the agony of suffering and death and of being forsaken. The destiny of God's People, of God's church, is from beginning to end one of striving with God and with men.

The cycle of Joseph stories faces us with yet another aspect of election. The beloved son of Jacob dreams visions of greatness which antagonize his brothers; he is rejected by them, sold as a slave. But again he is the chosen instrument of God's hand. He is lifted up to a position of honor and power and becomes in time of dire need the savior of a whole nation — and ultimately even of those who have betrayed him.

There is a moving scene in which he reveals his identity to his brothers: " And now do not be distressed, or angry with yourselves, because you sold me here; for God sent me before you to preserve life. . . . So it was not you who sent me here, but God; and he has made me a father to Pharaoh, and lord of all his house and ruler over all the land of Egypt." (Gen. 45:5, 8.) The wickedness of the brothers was a means used by God to achieve his saving purpose. Not only Jacob's tribe but the foreign land of Egypt was delivered through Joseph, for Jacob " blessed " Pharaoh.

Is this not a parable of what God one day will achieve in Christ? The rejected lifted up to the highest place, God's hand leading in such a way that through the unfaithfulness of Israel salvation will be extended to the nations and finally to Israel itself?

When we look at the patriarchal stories as a whole, we see

how each figure embodies some aspect of Israel's calling, of its history with God, man, and nations. We see how the great themes of election, separation, mission run through all. We see how the one figure who leads and dominates the whole story is God. The way in which he revealed himself, in which he "spoke" to these men of old, remains hidden to us. But that his steps are seen in history, that Israel is certain of his hand guiding its destiny, is the message that these chapters, in their graphic way, are meant to convey. We have heard, most of us, these stories in Sunday school, and we have been enticed by them. Maybe our teachers have put the stories in strait jackets, to draw a little moral lesson from each of them. They are not meant to moralize. They are meant to show man-as-he-is wrestling with God, and God wrestling with man. Adults all too often leave these stories behind with their memories of Robin Hood and Cinderella. We need to give the stories back to our generation as a living Word of God to his church in all times.

CHAPTER **III**

God Sets Apart a People

"Now therefore, if you will obey my voice and keep my covenant, you shall be my own possession among all peoples; ... and you shall be to me a kingdom of priests and a holy nation." (Ex. 19:5–6.)

The deliverance from Egypt and the entrance into the Promised Land is the most significant event of Israel's history.

The Exodus — a Sign and Token

Israel's faith in Yahweh as the God who leads its history, as the God to whom it is bound by the unique relationship of the covenant, is grounded in this first saving act. And this event will be celebrated again and again both in poetry and prose.

Miriam's song, probably the most ancient in Hebrew literature, illustrates the fact. She takes a timbrel and dances: " I will sing to the Lord, for he has triumphed gloriously; the horse and his rider he has thrown into the sea." (Ex. 15:1.) In the ancient confession of faith mentioned before in relation to Abraham, we read: " A wandering Aramean was my father; and he went down into Egypt and sojourned there, few in number; and there he became a nation, great, mighty, and populous. And the Egyptians treated us harshly, and afflicted us, and laid upon us hard bondage. Then we cried to the Lord the God of our fathers, and the Lord heard our voice, and saw our affliction, our toil, and our oppression; and the Lord brought us out of Egypt with a mighty hand and an outstretched arm, with

44

great terror, with signs and wonders; and he brought us into
this place and gave us this land, a land flowing with milk and
honey." (Deut. 26:5–9.)

It is significant that this confession should be a statement of
fact: God has *done something* and the relationship thus established between him and his People brings forth from them a
response of faith and gratitude. It should be noted that the
second article of the Apostles' Creed, produced centuries later,
is likewise a statement of fact. In both cases, we have to do with
the saving God who enters history to redeem his People. On
these deeds of God our faith is built. The deliverance from
Egypt is evoked again and again by prophet and psalmist. Sometimes it is a stern reminder of God's mercy and Israel's ungratefulness: "When Israel was a child, I loved him, and out of
Egypt I called my son. The more I called them, the more they
went from me." (Hos. 11:1–2; see also Ps. 78:9–20.) At other
times it is recalled as a motive for trust and hope in the face
of distress and need, or a joyful reminder of God's faithfulness
and " steadfast love " (see Ps. 105; 106; 136).

The significance of the exodus is further illustrated when,
in the book of Revelation, John the Seer hears the saints singing
with one voice " the song of Moses, the servant of God, and
the song of the Lamb" (Rev. 15:3). These two great deliverances — the exodus under Moses and the new exodus through
Jesus — are that foundation on which the faith of God's People
and the faith of the church rests:

> " Great and wonderful are thy deeds,
> O Lord God the Almighty!
> Just and true are thy ways,
> O King of the ages!
> Who shall not fear and glorify thy name, O Lord
> For thou alone art holy.
> All nations shall come and worship thee,
> for thy judgments have been revealed."
>
> (Rev. 15:3–4.)

Nothing is said in Exodus of the period from Joseph's death to the time of Moses. Tradition holds that it was four hundred years (Gen. 15:13; see also Acts 7:6); and we read in Ex. 1:7 that "the descendants of Israel were fruitful and increased greatly; they multiplied and grew exceedingly strong; so that the land was filled with them." One might easily consider this as an overstatement, but historical research has thrown an interesting light on the background of the Exodus story. We know now that there were strong Semitic infiltrations into Egypt, and particularly in this Delta region, at the time of the Twelfth Dynasty (1992–1779 B.C.). Around 1720 the Hyksos, Asiatic invaders of Semitic origin, dominated Egypt and ruled it until they were overthrown in 1550 by the Theban prince Ahmose I. The Semites were slaughtered or reduced to serfdom. (On Egyptian history of these times, see W. F. Albright, *op. cit.*, p. 7, and "The Old Testament World," in Vol. I of *The Interpreter's Bible*.)

"Now there arose a new king over Egypt, who did not know Joseph. And he said to his people, 'Behold, the people of Israel are too many and too mighty for us.'" (Ex. 1:8–9.) Here begins a tragedy which has gone on to this day: an alien minority becomes too strong and is considered a threat to national safety. This leads to open or secret hostility against the unassimilated group. From the days of Pharaoh to the days of Hitler, Israel has been a standing question posed to the rulers of the nations. Is the problem only that of a minority? Of any alien way of living? Is the conflict, as Buber puts it, between the dynastic and the charismatic principle, between the settled people and the wandering "Habiru"? Or is a deeper explanation to be sought? Since Israel bears the marks of a people set apart by God and can therefore never be fully assimilated anywhere, must it remain the perpetual stranger? We read the ancient tale with new feeling when, in the "enlightened" twentieth century, we have seen Hitler exterminate six million Jews. Pharaoh was milder. There is an ongoing mystery of Israel, of Israel's sufferings, which we cannot take lightly, that runs through all history.

In the Biblical story, God keeps silence for a long time during these events. Yet God watches over his people. The story of the midwives, the story of Moses' childhood, are tokens of his care. The story of Moses exposed on the Nile in a basket " made of bulrushes and daubed . . . with bitumen and pitch," shows how God chooses the weak things to confound the strong. It also is meant to show the hostility of the powers of this world seeking to thwart God's plan of salvation. There is a striking similarity between this story and that of the baby Jesus in his cradle, pursued by the cruel and relentless hatred of Herod the Great.

" And the people of Israel groaned under their bondage, and cried out for help, and their cry under bondage came up to God. And God heard their groaning. . . . And God knew their condition." (Ex. 2:23–25.) God *heard* — God *knew their condition*. The God of the Bible is concerned with human suffering; he stands with the oppressed. Is that true only of Israel? We shall go more deeply into this question later, but let us note how here already, in these ancient stories, God appears as the righteous God who sides with the weak, with the persecuted.

Moses: Prophet and Mediator

The chosen instrument for his People's deliverance is Moses, the young Hebrew brought up at the Egyptian court, " instructed in all the wisdom of the Egyptians, . . . mighty in his words and deeds " (Acts 7:22).

In his killing of the Egyptian, Moses acts on impulse; he relies on his own strength and he is defeated. But the positive element in his behavior is that he has taken sides with his oppressed people. As a consequence, God puts him in training in the land of Midian. He becomes a shepherd like his fathers —

until the day of revelation comes. God appears to Moses in the
fire of the burning bush. How God's *call* comes to him cannot
be described; but he is called by *name* and to a *definite mission*.
" I have seen the affliction of my people . . . , and I have come
down to deliver them." (Ex. 3:7-8.) Moses is called, spoken to,
set apart, not for his own sake but that he might be the instrument of God's plan of deliverance. Now he goes forward in the
strength of God, moved by a power not his own.

I shall not attempt here to discuss the meaning of Yahweh:
" I am who I am," or " I will be what I will be." Whatever the
meaning of the name, Yahweh reveals himself as the Holy One
who is present, always and at every moment, actively present.
There is nothing static about the God of the Bible! Moses tries
to escape the call. Most servants of God have known this reaction of fear and awe. Nevertheless, God will use Moses' stammering tongue.

There is much that is dramatic in the prolonged struggle between this man, whose sole power lies in God's word, and
Pharaoh, the very embodiment of the powers that be. Whose
son will be slain? God's " first-born," Israel, or Pharaoh's heir
(Ex. 4:22-23)? We are, at this point, far from the New Testament. But the time will come when God's heir will let himself
be killed for the sake not only of his people but for the sake
of all the Pharaohs of the earth. But this time has not yet come,
and we must read the story as one of both grace and judgment.
Israel's enemies are God's enemies, and their destruction is celebrated by Israel as an unequivocal token of God's love for his
people:

> " Sing to the Lord, for he has triumphed gloriously;
>   the horse and his rider he has thrown into the sea."
>   (Ex. 15:21.)

The 136th Psalm, written centuries later, echoes Miriam's
wild song:

"O give thanks to the Lord of lords,
        for his steadfast love endures for ever; . . .
"to him who smote the first-born of Egypt,
        for his steadfast love endures for ever."
                                        (Ps. 136:3, 10.)

Special mention should be made here of the institution of the Passover as described in chs. 12 and 13 of Exodus. Every family is to kill a lamb, and when the family is not large enough, two households are to join and eat the lamb together. They are to take the blood and smear the doorposts and lintel with it, and eat the lamb roasted with bitter herbs and unleavened bread. They are to eat standing, as ready for departure, their loins girded, and sandals on their feet. On that night God will slay the first-born of the Egyptians, but will spare all houses marked with the lamb's blood. At dawn Israel will start her exodus to the Promised Land.

Several things should be noted about this Passover meal. First, it is a family meal, the father of the house being the celebrant. Secondly, it is to be repeated every year as "a memorial" of God's great deeds. "And when in time to come your son asks you, 'What does this mean?' you shall say to him, 'By strength of hand the Lord brought *us* out of Egypt, from the house of bondage.'" (Ex. 13:14.) The *us* is significant: all oncoming generations should look upon this deliverance as a thing done to and for them. God acts in time at specific points in history, but the grace thus bestowed is an ever-present reality, received as such by all the children of Israel in all subsequent generations.

"In every age," says Rabbi Gamaliel, Paul's teacher, "it is the duty of everyone to imagine that he himself fled from Egypt, for it is written (Ex. 13:8), 'Thou shalt show thy son in that day, saying, This is done because of that which the Lord did unto *me* when I came forth out of Egypt.' Therefore we are bound to give thanks, to extol, to praise, to glorify, to exalt, to honor, to laud, to elevate and pay homage to Him who has done these wonders for our fathers and for us all, who led us from bondage to freedom, from sorrow to joy, from sadness to festivity, from darkness to the great light, from slavery to redemption. Before him let us all say Hallelujah! " (Quoted by Wilhelm Vischer, *The Witness of the Old Testament to Christ*, translated by A. B. Crabtree, pp. 173–174. Lutterworth Press, London, 1949.)

Finally, the way in which the meal is celebrated reminds the Israelites that they are a pilgrim people on the march:

" The Passover is the sacrament of those who have escaped from an alien land to make their journey to their fatherland, wanderers between two empires, summoned and expelled from the kingdom of the world to watch and to wait and to hasten toward the Kingdom of God.

" ' The Passover is the most Messianic of all Israelite festivals,' and most clearly expresses the historical separation of the people of Israel for their salvation." (*Ibid.*)

This is reflected in the Gospel of John when the crucifixion is placed on the fourteenth of Nisan. This stresses the fact that Jesus is the new Passover lamb " who takes away the sin of the world." At the Last Supper, Jesus speaks of his death as the new covenant signed with his blood: the final judgment that comes upon the world will leave those who believe in him unharmed.

✤

The struggle of Moses all along is on two fronts: with Pharaoh, who embodies the powers that be, the world in its resistance to God, Egypt and its magicians; but also with his own people. The worst tragedy of slavery is that one can get accustomed to it. The Hebrew tribes are afraid and skeptical. They will more than once forget past hardships and look back to the fleshpots of Egypt. They have to be saved in spite of themselves. Hence, the great leader's aloneness. He is the mediator, standing before his people in God's name, pleading before God for his people. How poignant does this pleading sound: " Alas, this people have sinned a great sin; they have made for themselves gods of gold. But now, if thou wilt forgive their sin — and if not, blot me, I pray thee, out of thy book which thou hast written"! (Ex. 32:31–32.)

Moses' God is the Holy One, the Entirely Other, who appears in the burning bush, in a mountain of fire and smoke, the God whom no one can approach, whose glory man cannot see and live (see Ex. 33:17–23). And he is also, simultaneously, the God of mercy who at the tent of meeting speaks to Moses "face to face, as a man speaks to his friend" (Ex. 33:11). Only such paradoxical affirmations can express the mystery of God as infinitely distant, yet infinitely near.

As Moses by faith leads his people through the Red Sea and through the wilderness, as he faces the stubbornness of a "stiff-necked people," he indeed tastes something of the solitude and the suffering of God. As prophet and mediator Moses is one of the men of the Old Testament whose very existence already bears some of the marks of the Greater Deliverer to come. This is evident when Paul opens a new perspective for us by comparing Israel's crossing of the Red Sea to a "baptism into Moses." It is Moses' faith which under God opens the way from death to life, from servitude to freedom. And here again what is done is done for God's People as a whole, whatever their place or time. " I want you to know, brethren, that our fathers were all under the cloud, and all passed through the sea, and all were baptized into Moses in the cloud and in the sea, and all ate the same supernatural food and all drank the same supernatural drink. For they drank from the supernatural Rock which followed them, and the Rock was Christ." (I Cor. 10:1–4; see also Ex. 15:19–25; chs. 16; 17:1–7.)

These last words are difficult for many of us. How should we understand them? They suggest at least this need: Christ is the living water, the true manna which feeds our souls. It is he, hidden but present, who stands behind the mediator Moses and guides God's People through the wilderness. Is he not present from the beginning with the Father, engaged in his redeeming work? To say more would be useless speculation.

The Covenant

When Moses dies, having seen the Promised Land only from afar — and this too is meaningful — he leaves a people, built into a unit under God, committed to a new way of life. The foundation stone of this new order of life is *the covenant*. " And Moses went up to God, and the Lord called him out of the mountain, saying, ' Thus you shall say to the house of Jacob, and tell the people of Israel: You have seen what I did to the Egyptians, and how I bore you on eagles' wings and brought you to myself. Now therefore, if you will obey my voice and keep my covenant, you shall be my own possession among all peoples; for all the earth is mine, and you shall be to me a kingdom of priests and a holy nation.'" (Ex. 19:3-6.) The saving God speaks: he binds himself to a people by a contract.

This, at first sight, may appear legalistic. The Bible often uses legal concepts and language as a medium of stressing the relation of God with his People as a responsible relationship. A false legalistic interpretation of the language is, of course, always possible. Israel drifted, at times, into such a caricature of God's intention, and it was the task of the prophets, and later of Jesus, to combat this misconception. It is all the more important to understand the real significance of the covenant idea.

In the story of Creation, we have seen God entrusting the whole world to man's stewardship; but man betrayed the trust. Now God entrusts to the chosen People a land. He restores a bit of man's trusteeship, so that Israel may be a " sign " for the whole earth of his sovereign rule. Israel is to be for God " a kingdom of priests," " a holy nation."

Two kinds of covenant are practiced in Israel. The one presupposes an agreement between two equal partners, for example, when two tribes pledge themselves to mutual assistance, or as in the covenant between David and Jonathan. The other type of covenant is the " royal covenant ": the ruler declares his will to enter into a covenant with his subjects. Thus King David makes a covenant with the elders of Israel who acknowledge him as their king (II Sam. 5:3).

The covenant of God with Israel is *a royal covenant*. The whole initiative belongs to *God*. The act by which God solemnly declares that Israel will be his people and that he will be their God crowns the deliverance from Egypt. A permanent living relationship is established. " I bore you on eagles' wings and brought you to myself." (Ex. 19:4.)

" The great eagle spreads out his wings over his nestlings; he takes up one of them, a shy or weary one, and bears it upon his pinions until it can at length dare the flight itself and follow the father in his mounting gyrations. Here we have election, deliverance and dedication, all in one." (Martin Buber, *Moses*. East and West Library, Oxford and London, 1946).

" Now therefore, if you will obey my voice and keep my covenant, you shall be my own possession among all peoples; for all the earth is mine, and you shall be to me a kingdom of priests and a holy nation." (Ex. 19:5-6.)

Each term here is important. The covenant is due to God's initiative. Israel stands as a sign of a restored relationship with God. It has been set into this new relationship: no reason is given for God's free choice. The book of Deuteronomy will stress more explicitly that no virtue, no merit of any kind, justifies this act of God; it is an act of sheer grace and mercy: " For you are a people holy to the Lord your God; the Lord your God has chosen you to be a people for his own possession, out of all the peoples that are on the face of the earth. It was not because you were more in number than any other people that the Lord set his love upon you and chose you, for you were the fewest of all peoples; but it is because the Lord loves you, and is keeping the oath which he swore to your fathers." (Deut. 7:6-8.)

In the Exodus passage, the sole condition of the blessing that will ensue is that Israel keep the covenant, maintain the relationship. Then it will be God's " own possession " or " peculiar treasure." According to Buber, the Hebrew term means something that is withdrawn from the general property as a special donation. This would explain the reminder: " for all the earth is mine."

Buber points out that the word rendered by " priest " can also mean " those who are at the immediate disposal of the king, appointed by the king " in a secular court. Thus the " kingdom of priests " would mean the direct sphere of the king's rule, his retinue. On the other hand, a priest is also a man who stands in the immediate presence of God and there represents the people. Both interpretations signify that all children of Israel stand in an identical and immediate relationship to God as his pledged servants; that they stand there *for the world,* for the whole of mankind. They are to be " a holy nation," for God is *holy*. The etymological origin of the word is uncertain: does it suggest the " Wholly Other "? Men or things are holy if they are consecrated to God, set apart wholly for his service.

It is not quite accurate to say that God sets apart *a people;* it is rather the covenant with him that makes the scattered tribes *into* a People. He makes a People of those who were no people. A specific term is used in Hebrew and in Greek to designate the People of God, in contradistinction to the foreign " nations." It is God's gracious covenant that calls Israel into being, creates Israel *as a People*. So the new covenant sealed by Christ's death and resurrection will call into being a new People, the church. Paul applies to the Gentiles and to their entrance into the church the words of Hosea:

> " Those who were not my people
> I will call ' my people,'

> and her who was not beloved
> I will call 'my beloved.'"
> (Rom. 9:25; see Hos. 2:23.)

I Peter applies to the church the very words of Ex. 19:5–6:

"You are a chosen race, a royal priesthood, a holy nation, God's own people, that you may declare the wonderful deeds of him who called you out of darkness into his marvelous light." (I Peter 2:9.)

And the book of Revelation speaks of the believers as a kingdom of priests (Rev. 1:6) or a " royal priesthood."

Note that in both texts the royal priesthood includes *all believers*. The word " laymen " comes from the Greek *laos,* " people." God's People are *dedicated for* the service of God, set apart for the service of the King. It is one of the paradoxes of language that in English the word " layman " has come to mean a person who is not competent in a certain area of knowledge. To be a " layman " in medicine means to be ignorant of medical science. To apply this word to the members of the church today implies a negative judgment of their competence, not a positive acknowledgment of their calling! While it is true that the layman is generally not a theologian and by definition not a member of the clergy, this distinction should never depreciate the layman's calling. Every member of Israel and every member of the church is " holy," that is, set apart for the service of God as were the " saints " of the Pauline Epistles by the very fact that each belongs to God's People. As we study the law we shall see that God's claim is on the whole life of his whole People. We must recover again and again the full meaning of the affirmation that claims every Israelite as a member of the King's retinue, and that asserts the universal priesthood of the members of the church as a body of believers.

Moses calls together " the elders of the people." This is a representative assembly, according to the tribal custom of the time where every family is represented by its head. We shall see that the tribes assemble in this way for two purposes: common worship and common defense. They are linked by a common allegiance to God and pledged to help one another in times of danger. The word "assembly" (Greek *ekklēsia*) means "those who are called out," but called out for a definite aim and purpose.

The awe of God's call is expressed in the smoking mountain that no one save Moses can approach (Ex. 19:7–25). It is shown in the story of the covenant in Ex., ch. 24. Here the ritual takes on a different character. It is a "blood covenant." Moses sprinkles the people with one half of the blood of the sacrifice, and throws the other half on the altar. Then he takes "the book of the covenant" and reads it to the people. They promise to be obedient, and Moses says: "Behold the blood of the covenant which the Lord has made with you in accordance with all these words." (Ex. 24:8.) Moses takes with him seventy elders — the first "presbytery"! — and they go up the mountain: "and they saw the God of Israel; and there was under his feet as it were a pavement of sapphire stone, like the very heaven for clearness." (Ex. 24:10.) God himself is *never described* in the Bible: only the *pavement under his feet, or the train of his garment* (see Isa. 6:1).

"They beheld God, and ate and drank": a sacred meal is eaten, the first "fellowship meal" of God's People. It is an ancient custom to seal a covenant with a meal. We have seen an instance of this in the encounter of Abraham and Melchizedek. Now the meal takes place in the mysterious presence of Almighty God.

We cannot help wondering if the number of the elders, namely seventy, has not here a specific meaning. In the tradition of Israel the number seventy stands for the nations. Is not the choice of this number to express the fact that Israel stands before God in a representative capacity for the nations? If so, we have here one more proof that at the time this story was written, the men of God in Israel knew of the instrumental character of their vocation as God's " holy priesthood," both as the first fruit and as the token of God's great work of reconciliation. (In Luke's Gospel, Jesus, entering Samaria, sends out seventy disciples and the instructions given seem to imply a mission to the Gentiles. This is in contrast to the sending of the Twelve.)

In the time of Joshua, when a new generation of Israel is on the point of entering the Holy Land, we are told of a renewed covenant celebrated at Shechem (Josh., ch. 24). This time more stress is laid on the responsibility that Israel incurs by entering the covenant: " Choose this day whom you will serve." (Josh. 24:15.) And when the people pledge themselves to serve the Lord, Joshua declares: " You are witnesses against yourselves that you have chosen the Lord, to serve him." (Josh. 24:22.) And he puts up a stone as a "witness " of the pledge taken.

To be "called " implies an increased responsibility before God and men; election is a two-edged sword. This will be stressed in later times with increased vigor in the book of Deuteronomy when, recapitulating the story of Exodus, it puts in the mouth of God the warning: " See, I have set before you this day life and good, death and evil. . . . I call heaven and earth to witness against you this day, that I have set before you life and death, blessing and curse; therefore choose life, that you and your descendants may live, loving the Lord your God, obeying his voice, and cleaving to him." (Deut. 30:15, 19–20.) Do such passages express only an Old Testament conception of God? The New Testament certainly reveals more of God's mercy and grace. But it stresses with equal vigor that the privilege of belonging to the covenanted People lays on one a unique responsibility: judgment is to begin with the house of God (see I Peter 4:17).

Does not the church as a whole need to recover this deep awareness of being " the covenanted People " whose life, per-

sonal and corporate, is a life under God? This awareness finds
an impressive echo in the "covenant service" in use in the
Methodist Church. This service, first instituted by John Wesley,
is "for such as would enter or renew their covenant with God."
It is meant to be celebrated on the first Sunday of the year but
can also be used at other times as a service of dedication. After
reminding the congregation of what it means to have been ad-
mitted into the new covenant that Jesus Christ sealed with his
blood, the minister invites the people to join with him in an act
of adoration, of thanksgiving, and of confession. He then ex-
horts all present to take the yoke of Christ upon them, and says
in the name of all:

"O Lord God, Holy Father, who hast called us through
Christ to be partakers in this gracious covenant, we take upon
ourselves with joy the yoke of obedience, and engage ourselves,
for love of thee, to seek and do thy perfect will. We are no
longer our own, but thine."

Here all the people join and say:

"I am no longer my own, but thine. Put me to what thou
wilt, rank me with whom thou wilt; put me to doing, put me
to suffering; let me be employed for thee or laid aside for thee,
exalted for thee or brought low for thee; let me be full, let me
be empty; let me have all things, let me have nothing; I freely
and heartily yield all things to thy pleasure and disposal.

"And now, O glorious and blessed God, Father, Son, and
Holy Spirit, thou art mine, and I am thine. So be it. And the
covenant which I have made on earth, let it be ratified in
heaven. Amen."

CHAPTER IV

God Is Lord: The Charter

*"Make thy face shine upon thy servant,
and teach me thy statutes. . . .*
*"Thy testimonies are righteous for ever;
give me understanding that I may live."*
(Ps. 119:135, 144.)

When we speak of the law, we are tempted to think immediately of rabbinic legalism and of Paul's letter to the Romans with its contrast between the law that kills and the gospel that saves. At the beginning of the Christian era, the law tended to be thought of as a way to salvation, a means by which men could earn the approval of God. This is not the sin of Judaism alone. In the history of the church, there are recurrent tendencies to replace God's grace by man's good deeds, to abandon salvation by faith for salvation through works. Nothing seems harder for man's natural pride than to accept the fact of God's gratuitous forgiveness. A wrong interpretation of the Old Testament has often led to a type of legalism in which moral achievement becomes a condition rather than a fruit of salvation. When the living relationship with God grows weak, we become legalistic. But it is unfair to oppose the Old Testament to the New Testament as though it were mere "law," as opposed to grace.

"I am the Lord Your God"

When we study earnestly the origin of law in the Hebrew tradition, we have a quite different picture: it is the *saving God*

59

who makes a covenant with his People. His act of salvation lays the foundation for the new relationship: *You are my chosen People and I am your God.* The law is the charter of the new society that God calls into being, the guardian of the God-given life and freedom.

We have seen in the background of Israel's consciousness of God a set of broken relationships, with God, with neighbor, and with the created world. The covenant is made by God's initiative and is designed to restore communion with him and to restore community among men. He sets apart a people who will acknowledge his sovereignty. He reveals to them *the laws of life.* He lays down the only conditions on which this society can stand. He has to do with the sinful, fallen nature of man: therefore, the law is like a boundary drawn round the rescued people. Violating the boundary will break the relationship, will mean falling back into enslavement to the powers of this world. It will mean death. Therefore, the repeated " Thou shalt not."

Because it is God's redeeming action that creates a new community, sin against one's neighbor is a sin against God. Because he has again entrusted this community with the stewardship of a bit of land, of a part of his creation, misuse of the land is a sin against God. There is a revealed will of God which embraces all realms of life. This is the concrete meaning of the law.

Social as well as personal ethics are rooted in Israel's living relationship with God. There is not a " social " versus an " individual " gospel: for Israel an individual gospel is inconceivable. The whole life of the tribe is involved in this new relationship. The ethic can never be detached from its spiritual root: it is grounded in God's will; it is Israel's response to his acts of mercy.

Many of our Christian liturgies leave out the preamble to the Ten Commandments: " I am the Lord your God, who brought you out of the land of Egypt, out of the house of bondage." (Ex. 20:2.) It is felt that the event thus described has little meaning for twentieth-century Christians. But this cuts the law from its foundation in God's redeeming action. In the Old as in the New Testament, it is God's grace manifested in an act of salvation that calls forth man's faith and obedience. The prophets will insist that the fundamental sin of Israel is not in the breaking of this or that commandment, but in the sin of ungratefulness: in trespassing the law it has rejected God's love manifested in its whole history.

The claim of the Lord is one of exclusive allegiance. "You shall have no other gods before me." (Ex. 20:3.) Here the strongest monotheism is affirmed. God cannot be represented in any material form. All idolatry is excluded. This is very impressive when we remember how all surrounding cultures worshiped their gods in human or animal form. Some scholars have tried to prove that monotheism was unknown to ancient Israel, and was initiated later by the great prophets of the eighth century. We believe this theory to be quite unwarranted. It may be that while God was the one God of Israel, the gods of other peoples were still thought of as having real existence. But prophets refer to the wilderness period as the time when Israel knew of only one God, namely, Yahweh. (See Hos. 2:1-3; 11:1-2; Jer. 2:2.) Israel's "prostitution" to other gods coincides with its settlement in Canaan.

During their stay in Egypt, the Israelites knew, and perhaps shared in, the worship of many gods represented in animal form. This is probably the explanation of the story of the golden calf. But even in Egypt, in Moses' time, there was an attempt to restore a purer religion. (On this point, see Albright, *op. cit.*)

Moses is shown in the Biblical story as the one who breaks completely and consciously with the Egyptian tradition, and to whom the "God of the fathers" reveals himself. We must take seriously the fact of this revelation. Moses' struggle to establish in Israel this purer faith, already known in the earlier nomadic period, is shown in the wilderness stories. The very purity of

this faith makes it hard for the people to accept. As soon as
Moses goes away, the people turn to Aaron: " Up, make us gods,
who shall go before us." (Ex. 32:1.) Israel wants a god that it
can "see," a god that will be "at its disposal" (an expression
of Martin Buber). It wants a visible symbol for security. Israel's
idolatry takes a crude form. At bottom it expresses a longing
which is deeply rooted in the human heart: we want a god we
can " see " or " feel," a god who should be ever ready to answer
our requests. Yahweh is not at his people's disposal. He is the
Almighty, invisible God, who speaks and acts when it pleases
him, the God wrapped in cloud and smoke, whose throne in the
Tabernacle cannot be occupied by any visible image.

The problem of idolatry goes deeper than material representa-
tion. Idolatry means putting anyone or anything above God or
on a level with him in our allegiance. The Bible insists from
beginning to end that we cannot have two masters. Our real
God is *that for which we live:* " For where your treasure is,
there will your heart be also." (Matt. 6:21.)

The warning "You shall have no other gods before me "
keeps its full significance when translated into contemporary
terms. Our modern world is full of idols in this sense: ourselves,
our " way of life " (meaning our ideology), money, power, success. Let us remember that we are very often able to pay lip
service to God while our true allegiance is elsewhere: our secret
desire is the real center around which our lives are built.

We have already seen that the law embraces the whole of
life. This is a common feature of ancient religions, and particularly so in the tribal system, where religious and social customs
are handed down from generation to generation as one total
view of life. Even in the developed written codes in use at this
era in Egypt and Babylon, law is seen as of divine origin, and it
includes both ethical and ritual prescriptions. Where, then, lies
the unique character of Mosaic law? It has borrowed many of
its elements from codes already in existence, as is obvious, for

instance, when one compares the Israelite with the Hammurabi Code. Also we find many layers in the Mosaic legislation, corresponding to different stages in Israel's life as it moves from the seminomadic period to settled agricultural and urban conditions.

But revelation does not mean that God dictates his will, as it were, *ex nihilo*. He uses human material, and this material is sifted and set in new perspectives. The uniqueness of the Mosaic legislation lies first of all *in the character of the God who reveals himself to his People*. We have already stressed the fact that this character can be described under three headings: holiness, righteousness, and mercy. Israel is "holy" because God is holy; it is set apart as God's exclusive possession. God's righteousness implies right relationships with God and neighbor; it implies justice. God's mercy, shown in his patience toward a rebellious people, means that Israel too is called upon to practice mercy. "Vengeance" belongs to God alone.

The monarchs of the great Asian empires promulgated law in their own "divine" right. No king of Israel will ever dare to do this; he stands under God's law. God allows no partiality: the law is binding for all, in all its parts. This is shown as well in the stern "You shall not " of the Decalogue as in the repeated "I am the Lord," which follows every commandment in Lev., ch. 19. The holy God establishes Israel's order of life, and determines both civil and sacred law.

The Basic Laws of Community Life

The second part of the Decalogue regulates work, and rest, and human relationships.

These relationships begin in the inner circle of the family. The authority of the father and husband stands unquestioned in patriarchal times. Yet father and mother are considered as one where the children are concerned: " Honor your father and your mother, that your days may be long in the land which the Lord your God gives you." (Ex. 20:12; see also ch. 21:15, 17;

Prov. 1:8.) The authority of the parents is a delegated authority, as is all authority in Israel: it is under God. The condemnation of adultery stresses the God-ordered oneness of husband and wife. The family unit stands in a wider unity, that of the tribe, of the covenanted People. Within the covenant all are "brothers" or "neighbors." Murder, stealing, blackmailing, envy will destroy community, and therefore they are condemned.

The character of the Holy God of Israel is revealed in Israel's concept of man. (See Walther Eichrodt's *Man in the Old Testament*, Henry Regnery Company, 1951, and his *Theologie des Alten Testaments*, J. C. Hinrich, Leipzig, 1935–1939, for the following considerations.) Because man is God's creature, made in his image (Gen. 9:6), human life is sacred and there is in Israelitish law an awareness of human dignity unparalleled elsewhere. Human life is always considered more precious than property. Thus willful murder is punished by death, but never stealing, as would frequently be the case in other legislation.

The slave is considered a person, though in the ancient world generally he is considered a piece of property. Mutilation is forbidden. The Hebrew, if enslaved for debts, shall be released on the seventh year. We are faced here, of course, with a fundamental distinction: the obligations of brotherhood are limited to the members of the tribe and to the strangers who live on its soil. Prisoners of war, members of other tribes or nations, can be enslaved for life. The gospel of Jesus will extend the concept of brotherhood to all human beings. But given these limits, Israelitish law shows in a striking way God's concern for both justice and mercy. God stands as the defender of the defenseless: of the poor, the widow, the orphan, the stranger. "You shall not wrong a stranger or oppress him, for you were strangers in the land of Egypt. You shall not afflict any widow or orphan. If you do afflict them, and they cry out to me, I will surely hear their cry; and my wrath will burn." (Ex. 22:21–24.)

We could still learn a good deal from the commandment,

"The stranger who sojourns with you shall be to you as the native among you, and you shall love him as yourself; for you were strangers in the land of Egypt: I am the Lord your God." (Lev. 19:33, 34.) Let us substitute for the word "stranger" the word "refugee" and remember the present plight of refugees in so many lands! Let us remember all the social exclusions we practice toward those of different social standing, or of different race! Old Israel was in the early times of its history a classless society, and it never fully lost its awareness of the equality of all men under God, however much it sinned against that principle.

God's concern for the poor is further expressed in the law that forbids one to exact interest for money lent to another member of the tribe. The law that forbids keeping a man's garment as pledge after sunset adds: "For that is his only covering, it is his mantle for his body; in what else shall he sleep? And if he cries to me, I will hear, for I am compassionate." (Ex. 22:25–27.) Here equity is merged with mercy. God's children are entitled to a minimum standard of living, and woe to those who exploit them! These laws take on contemporary significance when one thinks of the appalling poverty that still prevails among great masses of people in Asia and elsewhere, and of the terrific abuses of usury. The same social concern is expressed in the order to give a man his hire on the day he earns it, and in the regulations about harvesting: the forgotten sheaf, olive, or grape should be "for the sojourner, the fatherless, and the widow" (Deut. 24:19–22; see also Ruth, ch. 2).

Stewards of God's Property

One of the most interesting aspects of Israelitish law is its conception of land and property. Because God is the sole real proprietor of all earthly goods, the right of property is never an absolute one, as is the case in Roman law and in many modern codes. The central affirmation is that the earth belongs to God:

"All the earth is mine." (Ex. 19:5.)

The story of Creation shows that God called man to be his steward on earth. The covenant restores in Israel this lost sense of *stewardship*. Israel is to be given a *land,* a blessed land of "milk and honey." Every tribe, every clan is to be given a portion of this land; thus the land appertaining to each family is a direct gift of God: it should not be alienated. When King Ahab offers money to Naboth for his vineyard, Naboth answers, "The Lord forbid that I should give you the inheritance of my fathers" (I Kings 21:3). This is not a sentimental attachment to property. It is the reverence of the Israelite for God's holy will: it is He and no other who entrusted to Naboth's fathers that definite piece of property.

The Jubilee laws safeguard the right of property by requiring that every fifty years the land return to its original owners. At the same time they are reminded that they are only God's tenants, that they remain pilgrims on earth: "The land shall not be sold in perpetuity, for the land is mine; for you are strangers and sojourners with me." (Lev. 25:23; see also Lev. 25: 25-28.) God's People are to think of themselves as strangers and sojourners even in the Land of Promise! It is worth noting that this right to redeem the land is limited to *rural* property. There is a God-given link between a family and the land entrusted to it, but this does not apply in the case of city houses (see Lev. 25: 29-30). These laws have a deep theological significance. The only proprietor of the land and of all earthly goods is *God*. We are responsible to him for our use of property.

This right of God finds expression in the cult in the offering of the first fruits of the earth, of the first-born of the cattle. This is more than an act of thanksgiving: it is an acknowledgment that the earth and all its products are God's (see Ex. 23:19; 34:26; Deut., ch. 26). Man's relation to God is conceived as that of a tenant who gives to the owner part of the produce. And God cares for his land. The Sabbath is meant as a rest for men and cattle; so is the Sabbatical year meant to be a year of rest for the soil. This is a safeguard against ruthless exploitation. We have examples in history of the consequences such exploitation can have, leading to the destruction of natural resources and even depriving a whole population of its livelihood.

God the Lord of Time and Seasons

God is not only the Lord of space, he is the ordainer of time, who made day for work and night for rest, who set the seasons (see Ps. 104:19–23). This is the meaning of the laws on the Sabbath and on the yearly festivals. Certain moments in Israel's life are set apart for God, reminders that he is the creator and maintainer of life as well as the Lord of history. These institutions in their present Biblical form express both a social and a theological concern. The Sabbath marks the rhythm of life as one of work and rest; thus God's blessing lies on both. The social aim of the law is expressed in Ex. 23:12: " Six days you shall do your work, but on the seventh day you shall rest; that your ox and your ass may have rest, and the son of your bondmaid, and the alien, may be refreshed." And knowing the human heart and the farmer's temptation, Ex. 34:21 is even more specific: " In plowing time and in harvest you shall rest."

The Decalogue gives to this commandment a theological basis. In the Deuteronomy version of the Decalogue the argument is historical: every Sabbath should be a reminder of the great deliverance from the Egyptian yoke (Deut. 5:15). In the Exodus version the basis is, one might say, metaphysical and eschatological: Israel's rest reflects God's rest on the seventh day of Creation (Ex. 20:11). It announces the great rest to come, when God's People will partake forever of God's rest.

For Israel the rest comes on the seventh day, after six days of work. The Christian church has made the Lord's Day the first of the week. For us the day of deliverance is the day of the resurrection. The week's work is now under the sign of Christ's victory, it is to be seen in the light of the resurrection. At the same time the Lord's Day keeps the Sabbath's eschatological significance; it points to the final resurrection and to the rest of the Kingdom. We have rejected, most of us, the legalistic interpretation of the Sabbath because Jesus condemned it. But have we not all too often missed both the social and the theological significance of the Lord's Day?

"God," writes Professor Vischer, "desires . . . to liberate [his creatures] from their own 'activism,' that they may be free to adore his marvelous works" (*op. cit.*, p. 193). Israel gathers to offer the first lambs of the flock, the first sheaves of the harvest, and to give thanks after the ingathering of fruits and crops. But in the tradition of Israel, each feast is connected also with the great events of Israel's history. The spring festival beginning with the Passover meal, and followed by the Feast of Unleavened Bread, commemorates the deliverance from Egypt. But as the Jews stand and eat in haste they also remind themselves that they are the pilgrim people — ever on the march toward the Kingdom of God. The Feast of Pentecost is equally linked with the deliverance from Egypt. In later days water will be poured on the altar as a reminder of the rock in the wilderness and as a prophecy and token that one day the living water of the Spirit will flow from the Temple and revive the world (see Ezek., ch. 47).

The Feast of Ingathering, or Tabernacles, or Booths, is first of all a time of thanksgiving, but it is also meant as a reminder of the wilderness period when Israel lived under tents. The tenth day of the same month is to be a solemn Day of Atonement for the sins of all Israel. (See Ex. 23:14–17; Deut., ch. 16; Lev., ch. 23; also Lev. 16:29–30, and Neh., chs. 8; 9. The ritual laws in Leviticus in their present form represent a later stage of development.) Through all the rhythm of the year, Israel is thus reminded that God is Lord of the earth and Lord of history.

The Christian church has taken over this ancient tradition

and established the liturgical year to remind the "new Israel" of the great deeds of God in Christ: the incarnation, crucifixion, resurrection, and ascension of our Lord, and the baptism of the Spirit. Days are set apart for fasting or for thanksgiving as reminders of these great deeds.

The Christian festivals also have an eschatological meaning. Each one looks both backward and forward, to what God has done and to what he will do. Advent announces his coming in the flesh and his coming in glory; Easter, the victory achieved and the resurrection to come. Ascension is the glorious enthronement of our King in heaven, announcing the day when he will be Lord of all, and "every knee will bend before him." Pentecost manifests the breaking into this world of the new world, of God's Kingdom, the earnest of which is given by the Spirit.

The parallel with Old Testament festivals is a striking one, and should warn us not to dismiss lightly the Christian festivals, nor to turn them into profane occasions for holiday. At the same time, Christian freedom should exclude any legalistic interpretation. We are no longer bound to times and seasons: "One man esteems one day as better than another, while another man esteems all days alike. Let every one be fully convinced in his own mind." (Rom. 14:5.) The setting apart of certain times would not achieve its aim if it did not make God's deeds an even deeper reality in our daily life. The Psalms invite us to laud God's glory every day and to rejoice every morning in his salvation. The spiritual discipline to which Israel is submitted is not a way to salvation. It is a constant reminder that God's People have only one function on earth: to worship and glorify him, to love him with all their hearts, with all their souls, and with all their might (see Deut. 6:5).

The sacrificial laws show Israel's deep consciousness of sin as that which separates man from God. While sacrifices are ordained by God, we are reminded again and again that they are of no avail without a change of heart. For a Christian these sacrifices are " a shadow of things to come," a revelation of the depth of our lostness and need.

What lessons can we draw today from the ancient laws of Israel?

First of all, that our whole life is to be a life under God. Worship is at the center of Israel's life, but it is conceived as a means of sanctifying the whole of life, of placing the total existence of the community under God's sovereignty and guidance. This is certainly one of the things we need to relearn. Nothing is " profane," as opposed to " sacred," in a Christian's life. We cannot indulge in a Sunday religion that has no word to say about our daily tasks in family, school, or business. We are answerable to God for our relationships both in church and community.

Furthermore, modern society in its complexity raises many problems for which no direct answer can be found in the Bible. We are given, not a comprehensive, timeless code of ethics, but a living God who speaks in history. Yet some guiding lines emerge: there is a Biblical view of man, and of the sacredness of human life; of the responsibility of the members of the community for one another; of the specific duty of those entrusted with authority in the family or the group; of the use of property and the use of time; of work and rest. All these remain in force for our day.

CHAPTER V

God's People Get Settled

"Beware lest you say in your heart, 'My power and the might of my hand have gotten me this wealth.'" (Deut. 8:17.)

The march through the desert is looked upon by later authors as a time of both *testing* and *blessing*. It was a time when Israel depended wholly upon God for its life, its nurture, its very existence.

A Time of Training and Testing

The stories of Exodus and Numbers tell of a stiff-necked and murmuring people, who more than once look back with longing to the fleshpots of Egypt: "We remember the fish we ate in Egypt for nothing, the cucumbers, the melons, the leeks, the onions, and the garlic; but now our strength is dried up, and there is nothing at all but this manna to look at." (Num. 11:5–6.) The road to independence is hard and strenuous; the Promised Land seems to vanish in the distance. It requires all the faith of Moses to move the people forward. There are crises when all seems lost: the relapse into Egyptian paganism and the making of the golden calf; the torments of hunger and thirst; the fears and the defeats.

Yet looking back on that period the prophets will speak of Israel's first love:

71

> " I remember the devotion of your youth,
>   your love as a bride,
>   how you followed me in the wilderness,
>   in a land not sown.
>   Israel was holy to the Lord,
>   the first fruits of his harvest.
>   All who ate of it became guilty;
>   evil came upon them,
> > > says the Lord."
> > > > (Jer. 2:2–3.)

A similar picture is drawn by Hosea:

> " When Israel was a child, I loved him,
>   and out of Egypt I called my son.
>   The more I called them,
>   the more they went from me;
>   they kept sacrificing to the Baals,
>   and burning incense to idols.
> " Yet it was I who taught Ephraim to walk,
>   I took them up in my arms;
>   but they did not know that I healed them.
>   I led them with cords of compassion,
>   with the bands of love,
>   and I became to them as one
>   who eases the yoke on their jaws,
>   and I bent down to them and fed them."
> > > (Hos. 11:1–4.)

The prophets are aware that in spite of Israel's many rebellions, it was during the wilderness period that its fidelity to Yahweh was purest and loftiest. Israel had only one God, and its life was dependent upon him alone. It walked the hard path of faith and obedience. These were the pilgrim People on their march toward the Promised Land. They learned to " walk with God " and experienced his faithfulness amidst the hardest trials.

In one of the most beautiful chapters of the book of Deuteronomy, Moses challenges Israel to " remember " and " beware." This book was composed in its present form in the seventh cen-

tury B.C. Some of its parts are ancient, as we have already seen.
It is a kind of retrospective account put into the mouth of Moses.

" And you shall remember all the way which the Lord your God has
led you these forty years in the wilderness, that he might humble
you, testing you to know what was in your heart, whether you
would keep his commandments, or not. And he humbled you and
let you hunger and fed you with manna, which you did not
know, nor did your fathers know; that he might make you know
that man does not live by bread alone, but that man lives by everything that proceeds out of the mouth of the Lord. Your clothing did
not wear out upon you, and your foot did not swell, these forty years.
Know then in your heart that, as a man disciplines his son, the Lord
your God disciplines you. . . .
   " Take heed lest you forget the Lord your God, by not keeping his
commandments and his ordinances and his statutes, which I command you this day: lest, when you have eaten and are full, and have
built goodly houses and live in them, and when your herds and
flocks multiply, and your silver and gold is multiplied, and all that
you have is multiplied, then your heart be lifted up, and you forget
the Lord your God, who brought you out of the land of Egypt, out
of the house of bondage. . . . Beware lest you say in your heart,
'My power and the might of my hand have gotten me this wealth.'"
(Deut. 8:2-5, 11-14, 17.)

   When the Northern Kingdom in later years falls a prey to
idolatry and prostitutes itself to foreign gods, the prophet Hosea
will see a new exile, a new " wilderness," as the only means by
which God may again " speak to the heart " of Israel and open
for it a new " gate of hope." (See Hos., ch. 2.)
   Israel is said to have spent forty years in the wilderness. Moses
had spent forty years in exile in Midian, and encountered there
the living God of his fathers. Elijah later walked forty days to
Horeb before he heard God's " still small voice " (I Kings
19:12). Jesus still later spent forty days " in the wilderness," before entering his ministry. In each case, the forty days stand for
a period of both probation and revelation. It is always a solitary

way which cuts off the servant of God from his earthly moorings and throws him back on God alone, on his word and his mercy. It is often a time of preparation, of "separation" preceding a return to the world.

The "wilderness" can take many forms in the life of God's church and of the individual Christian. It can be the isolation of a minority church exposed to the hostility of its surroundings, of a confessing church in times of persecution. It can be, for the individual, the solitude of the sickbed, or of the prison camp. It can mean that all earthly securities are taken away. Or again, it can be the lonely struggle to find and accept God's will. In all cases, it is a test of the reality of our faith in God, meant to lead us to a deeper encounter: "Know then in your heart that, as a man disciplines his son, the Lord your God disciplines you." (Deut. 8:5; see also Heb. 12:1–11.)

Entering the Promised Land

The wilderness experience is followed for Israel by the conquest of the Promised Land. Here again the hand of God leads powerfully, and Joshua is the chosen instrument who brings to its fulfillment the task started by Moses. The story of the conquest related in The Books of Joshua and Judges has its dark sides, which puzzle the modern reader: the cruelty of the conquerors; the command, so emphatically repeated in Deuteronomy, to destroy utterly the defeated populations. Here we must take into account the practices of those times. What had been consecrated to a god shared in the power of that god. It had therefore to be utterly destroyed; it was taboo. This was a common belief. Furthermore, the destructions were less drastic than certain passages seem to imply. For example, Judg. 2:21–22 says, " I will not henceforth drive out before them any of the nations that Joshua left when he died, that by them I may test Israel, whether they will take care to walk in the way of the Lord as their fathers did, or not." Moreover, subsequent events in some measure justify the severity of the conquest. Israel undergoes a dangerous process of assimilation. The People of the covenant are in danger of becoming " like all other nations," and of forsaking their mission.

The conquest continues over about three centuries. Not only do the Canaanites remain firmly established in some parts of the country (Judg., chs. 1; 2), but new invaders from the outside threaten the Hebrew tribes again and again. These invaders are wild, camel-riding tribes coming from Arabia on the east, or the well-organized Philistine army which invades Palestine from the west, by land and sea, around 1187 b.c. The Philistines very nearly take over the country and will not be finally overthrown until the time of David, two centuries later.

During this whole period, Israel is less a nation than a federation of tribes linked up by a cultic and military covenant. It is only their faith in Yahweh that holds them together. In times of danger the tribes are summoned in the name of Yahweh by a " charismatic leader " who acts as military chief. (This term, first launched by German scholars, underlines the call of these men to a specific and temporary task.) These chiefs are called judges, probably because their prestige as military leaders made them arbiters in conflicts arising within or between the tribes. Also, through them the judgment of God is executed on his enemies.

This charismatic element is characteristic of the whole period. The institutions of church and state are still very weak. The Spirit of God comes down on those whom God calls, and endows them with the necessary power to fulfill their missions. (See Judg. 11:29; 14:5-6, 19.) This may be the place to note that in the Old Testament the Spirit of God often comes down on a man so that he may fulfill a specific God-given function in the community. We see the Spirit coming down thus on the judges, fitting them to lead God's People to victory, and on Saul and David after their anointment as kings of Israel (see I Sam.

10:9–10; 16:13). This functional role of the Spirit is also shown in the account in Exodus, where God fills with his Spirit the craftsmen who are to work on the furnishings and vestments of the Temple. They are "to devise artistic designs, to work in gold, silver, and bronze, in cutting stones for setting, and in carving wood" (Ex. 31:1–5). Here the Spirit is given to the worker that he may create beauty, and that God may be thereby glorified. As we go on, we shall see the charismatic gifts being superseded by the institution. Is not this also a recurring evolution — perhaps an unavoidable one — in the life of the church?

Where Is Thy God?

When the tribes settle in Canaan, they undergo a total change of condition. They had led a seminomadic, isolated life. They had been Yahweh's marching army, linked together by a common faith and a common goal. Now they are exposed to an utterly different type of civilization, to a far more advanced culture, and at the same time to a very crude and sensual kind of popular religion. The impact of these influences on the faith of Israel is already strongly marked in The Book of Judges, but its full effect will be felt in the time of the monarchy.

The first change the Hebrews undergo is in passing from a nomadic to a settled life. Before, they were shepherds, driving their flocks, free in their movements, like the wind of the desert. Now they become farmers, tied to the soil. This economic change soon raises a theological question: Is Yahweh, the wilderness God, the war God, also the God of the Canaanite soil? The Canaanite farmer worships the Baals as the gods of fecundity. Is it not safer to be on good terms with these divine protectors, so long settled in the land? Israel is thus led to compromise its faith, to make two parts in its life: Baal is the god of everyday life; but the People cry to Yahweh in times of dire need and danger (see Judg., ch. 2). This is at the heart of Israel's "prostitution" to the gods of the new land. It is illustrated by the story of the prophet Elijah. A terrible drought has devastated the land. The question arises: Who provides the rain, Yahweh or Baal? The victory of Elijah over the prophets of Baal proves that God is Lord over his creation and that there is no other god beside him. (See I Kings, ch, 18; Elijah's triumph was followed by a bloody slaughter. Maybe the story in ch. 19 should be understood as a protest against Elijah's somewhat crude view of God; see especially ch. 19:11–13.)

A century later the prophet Hosea had to fight the same fight. He voices God's comparison of Israel to an unfaithful wife: "She did not know that it was I who gave her the grain, the wine, and the oil." (Hos. 2:8; see the entire chapter.) This impact of Baalism throws light on the insistence with which the prophets later reminded Israel that God is the creator of all life, as truly as he is the saving God at work in their history.

A second aspect of Israel's change of condition is to be found in the political realm. We have seen that Israel started its common life as a cultic and military association of free tribes. They were pledged to help one another in case of attack, and God provided the leader who conducted the "holy war." The Ark was the rallying point, the sign that God himself led the army. The warriors were submitted to a strict moral discipline while in camp — they were "holy." When victory was won, they returned to their flocks and fields. The democratic feeling of the tribes is expressed in the parable of the trees that want a king: only the bramble consents to be elected (see Judg. 9:7–15). It is shown further in Gideon's reaction when the men of Israel ask him to rule over them: "I will not rule over you, and my son will not rule over you; the Lord will rule over you." (Judg. 8:23.)

But a time comes when Israel wants a king. When Samuel refuses, he receives the answer, "No! but we will have a king over us, that *we also may be like all the nations,* and that our king may govern us and go out before us and fight our battles"

(I Sam. 8:19–20). Thus begins the real tragedy of Israel: relying on God alone is too difficult; they want to be "like all the nations." Humanly speaking, the concern for a more stable political organization was reasonable. The constant threat of the Philistine kingdom made national unity a necessity. But the demands of the monarchical system were going to prove heavy: "These will be the ways of the king who will reign over you: he will take your sons and appoint them to his chariots and to be his horsemen, and to run before his chariots; and he will appoint for himself commanders. . . , and some to plow his ground and to reap his harvest. . . . He will take your daughters. . . . He will take the best of your fields." (I Sam. 8:11–14.) This is the voice of old Israel, of free Israel which knows the price of human power and greatness. And above all other voices we hear the voice of God saying, "They have rejected me from being king over them" (I Sam. 8:7).

Yet, God yields to the demand of his People. He consents to make a new beginning by appointing a king who will be his representative on earth, answerable to him for the way in which he fulfills the king's function. The king stands over Israel, but he stands under God. This is shown in the story of Saul. God's blessing rests on the young chieftain until the days come when he dares to trespass the limits assigned to a king and assumes duties reserved to the priest (see I Sam., ch. 13). A second time he breaks God's commandment by sparing the king of Amalek and allowing the people to take the sheep and oxen devoted to destruction (I Sam., ch. 15). According to modern standards, his sins seem mild! But he has put himself above the law of God, and this is his doom. The mad king is a tragic figure. His love for David is changed into hatred when David turns out to be his rival in successful warfare. Now it is David and no longer Saul who bears the visible signs of election. The rejected king ends in self-destruction.

Wherein lies David's greatness? Humanly speaking, he is a

very great king: he has put an end to Philistine domination, he has built Israel's unity, extended its borders, given it its capital, Jerusalem, the "City of David." His real greatness, though, seen in the light of Biblical revelation, lies not in his human achievements but in his awareness of the royal responsibility he carries as God's anointed. He stands in God's keeping and under God's judgment. So deep is his regard for God's anointed that he would not lay his hand on Saul when the defeated king lay at his mercy (see I Sam., chs. 24; 26). When he himself has sinned he accepts God's chastisement without complaint. We see here again that the men of God, and even the greatest among them, do not present us with an ideal picture of man; they are sinful beings. Their story is one of mercy and grace; but they know it (see II Sam., ch. 7). God "builds a house" for David; David is not worthy to build a house for God. He pays heavily for his mistakes. He will see his own house divided against itself, and he will flee for his life. And the seed of division and strife will bear its fruits one generation later: the unity of the kingdom, so wisely achieved, will be destroyed.

Power and Glory

With Solomon (961–922 B.C.), Israel reaches the peak of earthly glory. We are told that "King Solomon excelled all the kings of the earth in riches and in wisdom. And the whole earth sought the presence of Solomon to hear his wisdom, which God had put into his mind" (I Kings 10:23–24). This is no exaggeration: his fame spread far beyond his borders, as is shown by the story of the queen of Sheba. To this day, "King Suleiman" has remained a legendary figure in the Arab world. Solomon is allied by marriage with the Egyptian Pharaoh. His alliance with the king of Tyre opened for Israel wide possibilities of foreign trade. Copper mines were exploited and refineries opened, employing Phoenician methods. He erected a palace, the building of which is said to have required thirteen years, and many other houses. He built stalls for several thousand horses (see Albright, *op. cit.*, pp. 26–29). He organized a strong army with chariots. Above all, he built the Temple in Jerusalem. Let us note in passing that nothing was too beautiful to honor God: only the best (genuine) kind of material, stone, cedar, olive-wood, and gold, could be used.

All these buildings called for labor. We are told that " King Solomon raised a levy of forced labor out of all Israel " (I Kings 5:13). While this levy was temporary, Solomon also made a forced levy of slaves, drawn from the foreign peoples dwelling in the land (see I Kings 9:15–22). He did, in fact, what Pharaoh in other times had done to Israel.

When one reads the first ten chapters of I Kings, one sees how Israel was under the spell of this glorious reign, humanly speaking the high point of the United Kingdom. But this display of wealth and power was a denial of the pure religion of Yahweh and soon bore its bitter fruits. By the end of his reign, the old king drifted into idolatry, influenced by his foreign wives. The Biblical account presents us with the appalling number of a thousand wives and concubines, a harem that scarcely could find its equivalent even in Moslem history! His policies had other far-reaching consequences. Political alliances and a regular army are now the forces on which Israel relies for its safety. It has at last truly become "a nation like all the others"!

The social change is no less drastic. Old Israel was a classless society, with a strongly knit, corporate existence, and a deep sense of justice. Now we are faced with sharp contrasts of wealth and poverty. The country is ruled by the powerful and the rich at the expense of the common man. Finally, by the moving of the Ark to the royal city under David, and the construction of the Temple under Solomon, the priesthood has been tied to the throne, and a " state religion " is developing, bringing all the corruptions that state religions produce.

A crisis occurs immediately after Solomon's death. To the people who complain that his father's yoke was heavy, the young King Rehoboam answers by a threat: "My father chastised you with whips, but I will chastise you with scorpions." (I Kings 12:14.) The monarchy now pretends to stand in its own right. Rehoboam refuses to be a "servant" to his people (I Kings 12:7). Still less has he any thought of submitting himself to the law of God. A revolt breaks out, and the kingdom is split. The Northern Kingdom of Israel will go through a long succession of bloody palace revolutions. Its separation from the Davidic dynasty will involve the building up of "royal sanctuaries," and of an independent priesthood attached to them. The paganization of the Northern Kingdom will be a swift process. That kingdom will know times of earthly greatness, but of all its kings it will be said that they "did what was evil in the sight of the Lord." Israel's divine mission is forgotten. In spite of its numerous mistakes and apostasies, the little Kingdom of Judah will carry on the witnessing function of God's People until new and drastic siftings take place and God's People are again "unsettled" in order to be saved!

It may be useful at this point to give some chronological data. We shall adopt, in doing so, the figures given in the "Introduction to the History of Israel," by Theodore H. Robinson, in *The Interpreter's Bible;* Vol. I, referring the reader to that Introduction for further details:

Moses and Exodus	after 1500 B.C.
Entry Into Palestine	ca. 1350?
United Monarchy	ca. 1030–936
Divided Kingdom	936–721
Fall of Northern Israel	721
Fall of Judah	586
Return from Exile	538
Judah Under Persian and Greek Domination	538–167

Maccabean Revolt, Independence	
Restored	167–63
Roman Domination	63 B.C.
Destruction of Jerusalem	A.D. 70

We have dwelt at length with this crucial period of Israel's history because the problems it raises are recurrent ones in the history of the church.

"Assimilation" Versus "Separation" — *a Permanent Problem*

The attempt to transpose into our own situation the lessons learned by Israel in the period of life we have just described immediately raises a delicate point. Israel is both nation and church. It is in a unique position among the nations, as a society under God. Since Christ came, the new society under God is the church, and this society has no wholly separate life. Its members belong also to secular communities and groups. Therefore, the interpenetration of church and world takes on new forms. None of us would like to revive the times when attempts were made to build a theocracy, nor would we desire to have the secular power under the control of the spiritual power. Many of us, sharing Jesus' conviction that his Kingdom is not of this earth, are thankful that the Constantine era has come to an end. The official protection of the church by the state has been a costly affair, jeopardizing the purity of the gospel.

Yet, fundamentally, the problem of separation versus assimilation remains. It exists within the church as a community that is constantly tempted to adopt the ways and methods of the world. It exists in the relation of the church to the world, since we believe that the church has, as we shall later see, a prophetic function as the *watchman* in the city.

A sociological condition similar to the one Israel had to face arises whenever a primitive people are exposed to a more developed type of civilization: they are in danger of being absorbed — or annihilated. We have had examples of this in our Western conquests. We are faced today in Africa with the breakdown of tribal structures which all too often are not replaced in any constructive way. The individual, deprived of his ancient customs and the ethical standards prevailing in tribal society, is exposed to all the temptations of a secularized Western culture for which he is totally unprepared.

In the case of Israel, the attraction of popular paganism with its sexual crudities as well as the secular trends in the wealthy Canaanite towns was such that, humanly speaking, total absorption became a real threat. It was indeed the miracle of God that the Yahwistic faith survived. In many parts of the world today, the younger churches find themselves in a similar situation. They stand, a tiny minority, faced with a recrudescence of ancient religions and cultures on the one hand, with secular, materialistic ideologies on the other. Will they prove capable of survival? It depends on the vigor and depth of their faith and on their ability to build up *true community*. We must trust that, now as in olden times, God will not leave himself without witnesses, remembering that he has always chosen the weak things to confound the strong.

Does this mean that, claiming to be God's People, we should utterly reject the cultures that surround us, in order not to be contaminated by them? This is the position taken in Israel by the sect of the Rechabites: they stuck to the nomadic way of life and were pledged never to build houses, never to sow fields or to plant vineyards. (But even they, in times of war had to take refuge in Jerusalem! See Jer., ch. 35.) In modern times we had the example of Gandhi, attempting to boycott the machine, and exhorting India to revert to home spinning. Such attitudes are not only unrealistic. They seem to us un-Biblical. God did not leave Israel in the wilderness. He chose to lead his People to a country that stood at the very crossroads of ancient nations and cultures. He did not place them in an intellectual and spiritual vacuum. In fact, Biblical writers have found much of their material in the common treasure of wisdom of the ancient East. Yet all this has been sifted, purified, integrated in the fire of Yahweh's revelation and judgment. At the same time, thanks to its exposed position, Israel's outlook and hope could expand beyond its frontiers.

The problem, therefore, is not one of total assimilation as opposed to total rejection, but of the criteria by which we shall discern what to accept and what to reject. In the history of world missions the problem is a recurring one, and both extremes have fatal consequences. The question is one of what Paul would call " discernment of spirits " — a deep-rooted faithfulness to God's revelation as the criterion by which we shall test all things.

There is another aspect to the tribes' settling in Canaan. They soon lost the dynamic faith of a pilgrim People marching toward their goal. Outward security lessened their sense of God, their need of him, their dependence upon him: "Beware lest you say in your heart, 'My power and the might of my hand have gotten me this wealth.'" (Deut. 8:17.)

When a nation comes of age, it relies more and more on human power and efficiency to realize its aims. We are proud to be "self-made men," or a "self-made nation." Is this altogether bad? No, for it can lead us to a loftier, more disinterested love of God. We shall seek him for his own sake rather than for his gifts. But it can also mean, and all too often does mean, that we shift from a God-centered to a man-centered view of life where our real god becomes Man and his achievements, or the nation and state as the embodiment of these achievements. It is no longer the will of God that serves as the touchstone of our lives, but worldly success and efficiency.

As Israel was blinded by the sudden expansion of its power, its trade, its wealth, so are we in danger of being blinded by the astounding developments of our technical age. We shall come back to this in the next chapter. Not only God but human values are in danger of being pushed into the background. The Biblical writers give evidence, and our present civilization confirms it, that when we become man-centered instead of God-centered, possessions tend very soon to become more precious than life, especially the lives of other peoples. This means the exploitation of backward groups or races. It often means a feverish rush in which the higher values of life are neglected and finally forgotten.

Where should resistance to such trends be found if not in the church? But this implies that it, at least, will not be carried away by the slogans of the day. In the case of Israel, the real tragedy of the times was that " religion " had superseded " faith." Faith, in the religion of Yahweh, meant a personal relationship with, a total dependence upon, the living God of Israel. This faith implied a definite view of man-in-community. Religion, on the other hand, may answer man's search for security in another way. Its aim is to satisfy the need of man to be protected against adverse powers, and reassured as to his own destiny. Human nature is such that it will always attempt to escape from the commitments and risks of faith by seeking the appealing haven of religion. The prophets' function will be to smash all such security. No wonder that they are often, to the world, men with whom it is highly unpleasant to live!

CHAPTER **VI**

Watchmen in the City

" Upon your walls, O Jerusalem,
I have set watchmen;
all the day and all the night
they shall never be silent."
(Isa. 62:6.)

We have seen that in the early times of Israel's national life, its leadership had a charismatic character. When the monarchy becomes hereditary and throne and altar tend to be so closely associated that the priesthood becomes the servant of the state, God calls forth a new category of men: the prophets. It will be the task of the prophets to address king, priest, magistrate, and people in the name of the holy God of Israel.

God's Word Comes

The origins of prophecy are complex and partly obscure. At times the prophets seem to have constituted a special caste or guild. In Ahab's time we hear that there were hundreds of prophets in the Northern Kingdom, some in the service of Baal and some in the service of Yahweh. They often indulged in ecstatic manifestations which could degenerate into real frenzy (see I Kings 18:25–29). They were supposed to know the future, to have special powers to bring a blessing or a curse. Therefore, they were both respected and feared. (On this point, see the ancient story of Balaam, Num., chs. 22; 23).

The Biblical writings draw a sharp contrast between the false prophet who says what king and people *want to hear,* and the true prophet who is God's spokesman and can speak only the word given to him by God himself. Thus we see Elijah standing alone against all the prophets of Baal, and at the risk of his life. We see at the same time Micaiah, son of Imlah, alone against four hundred prophets who have prophesied victory. " And the messenger who went to summon Micaiah said to him, ' Behold, the words of the prophets with one accord are favorable to the king; let your word be like the word of one of them, and speak favorably.' But Micaiah said, 'As the Lord lives, what the Lord says to me, that I will speak.'" (I Kings 22:13–14.) It is no wonder that a prophet is a solitary figure. God's Word seldom coincides with the wishes of men.

At a later time Jeremiah will describe with bitter irony the attitude of the false prophets who fill the people with " vain hopes," who " speak visions of their own minds, not from the mouth of the Lord," who " say continually . . . , ' It shall be well with you '" (Jer. 23:16–17).

> " For who among them has stood in the council of the Lord
>   to perceive and to hear his word,
>   or who has given heed to his word and listened? . . .
>
>> " ' I did not send the prophets,
>>   yet they ran;
>>   I did not speak to them,
>>   yet they prophesied.' "
>>> (Jer. 23:18, 21.)

They are " dreamers." But the word of the Lord is " fire," " a hammer which breaks the rock in pieces" (Jer. 23:27–29).

The Roaring Lion

It must be clear from the outset that the power of the true prophet lies wholly in the word he is called to proclaim. He is bound to speak:

> " The lion has roared;
>   who will not fear?
>   The Lord God has spoken;
>   who can but prophesy? " (Amos 3:8.)

Who is the man who speaks like that? Not a prophet in the

technical sense, but an ordinary layman, a shepherd, a dresser of sycamore trees (see Amos 7:14–15). God has taken him from behind his flock and sent him to the Northern Kingdom to proclaim its doom. His task done, Amos goes back to his Judean desert and disappears from the scene of history. He is a " voice," nothing more; but this voice is God's voice.

How did this solitary herdsman gain such insights into world history? God opened his mind and gave him his message. God's call coming to a man always remains, in its essence, God's inexplicable secret. But we should see at the same time that Amos stands in the purest Yahwistic tradition. His is the holy God of Israel who cannot stand iniquity. And this man must have pondered in solitary meditation God's call to his People. He has gone down to the plain of Samaria, he has observed what was going on in the market place and at the gate of the city where the judges sit. The Northern Kingdom under Jeroboam is booming with prosperity, it has extended its frontiers, it feels strong and safe. But to the man of Tekoa all this outward success is of no avail. The fruit is rotten. He sees with scorn that there is no justice in the land. The Northern Kingdom has drifted away from the true faith. Its sanctuaries, with their gorgeous feasts, indulge in the worst kind of idolatry. Israel has forsaken its mission in and to the world. The wrath of God is kindled. He roars like a lion. His day will be not light but darkness, not blessing but judgment! And here comes the shepherd-prophet singing a lamentation as for a burial:

> " Fallen, no more to rise,
> is the virgin Israel;
> forsaken on her land,
> with none to raise her up." (Amos 5:2.)

We should try to visualize the picture of this " foreigner " from the south in his shepherd's cloth, standing amongst the crowd at the royal sanctuary on a great feast day and chanting his litanies of doom! Amaziah, the priest of Bethel, said to Amos, " O seer, go, flee away to the land of Judah, and eat bread there, and prophesy there; but never again prophesy at Bethel, for it is the king's sanctuary, and it is a temple of the kingdom " (Amos 7:12–13). In other words: " Foreigner, go home! What do you know about the problems of our state? Your offensive speeches are indeed misplaced! Leave us alone and we shall know how to manage our problems! " A prophet can eventually be killed. He cannot be sent home before he has said all he has to say.

It seems worth-while to study more closely the signs of decay that Amos discerns in the society of his time. The root of all evil lies for him in the fact that Israel has broken its covenant with Yahweh. We have seen that this covenant implied righteousness in human relationships; therefore, where there is no justice, God's name is taken in vain: " They sell the righteous for silver, and the needy for a pair of shoes — they . . . trample the head of the poor . . . ; they lay themselves down beside every altar upon garments taken in pledge." (Amos 2:6–8; see also Ex. 22:25–27.) Justice is corrupted. When rich and poor, friend and foe, are not given the same fair hearing in the courts of justice, something is rotten in the land. Official religion may attract thousands; but all this display of piety is of no avail:

> " I hate, I despise your feasts,
>   and I take no delight in your solemn assemblies.
> Even though you offer me your burnt offerings
>   and cereal offerings,
>   I will not accept them,
> and the peace offerings of your fatted beasts
>   I will not look upon.
> Take away from me the noise of your songs;
>   to the melody of your harps I will not listen.
> But let justice roll down like waters,
>   and righteousness like an ever-flowing stream."
>   (Amos 5:21–24.)

Never has the line been drawn more sharply between "religion" and faith in God. Man's instinctive need for spiritual reassurance and for security can be satisfied by outward ceremonies and "peace offerings." But the God of Israel is not interested in such emotional outlets. He wants obedience. He wants justice in the land. The merchant is answerable to him for falsifying measures, making "the ephah small and the shekel great," for dealing deceitfully with false weights. The speculator who is so impatient to resume business that he cannot wait for the end of the Sabbath or of the full moon is offending God (see Amos 8:4–6). One great cry runs through the whole Book of Amos: "You have turned justice into poison." (Amos 6:12.) Israel's covenant with God is broken from top to bottom: king, priest, and people have put their trust in money and success; they have drifted away from the faith as well as from the simple way of life of the fathers. They trust in their "own strength" (Amos 6:13). Therefore, they are doomed.

The startling fact is that while Amos' prophecies of impending doom seemed scarcely borne out by the facts when he spoke them, they were to come true about twenty years later. The Northern Kingdom was literally wiped off the map; its inhabitants were dragged into exile, and partly replaced by alien populations, under the thorough and cruel whip of Assyria.

God Pleads

The message of the northern contemporary of Amos, Hosea, is as stern, but with a different kind of appeal. It is the call of a man who knows by bitter human experience what it means to be abandoned and betrayed by the one he loves. God pleads with Israel as a husband pleads with his adulterous wife. The image is a daring one. Of all possible metaphors, Hosea uses those which express the closest personal relationship: the image of the husband and that of the father (see Hos., chs. 1 to 3; 11:1). Yet no human language is deep enough to express God's love and suffering for his People. Hosea's message goes farther than that of Amos: chastisement is not an end in itself, but a means of speaking to the unfaithful one to bring her back:

> "Therefore, behold, I will allure her,
>   and bring her into the wilderness,
>   and speak tenderly to her.
> And there I will give her her vineyards,
>   and make the valley of Achor a door of hope.
> And there she shall answer as in the days of her youth,
>   as at the time when she came out of the land of Egypt."
>   (Hos. 2:14-15; Achor means "trouble.")

Exile is a means of reconquering the heart of Ephraim. Yet, a struggle goes on in the very heart of God:

> "How can I give you up, O Ephraim!
>   How can I hand you over, O Israel! . . .
> My heart recoils within me,
>   my compassion grows warm and tender.
> I will not execute my fierce anger,
>   I will not again destroy Ephraim;
> *for I am God and not man,*
>   the Holy One in your midst,
>   and I will not come to destroy."
>   (Hos. 11:8-9.)

The "otherness" of God, which struck the Israel of old with fear and awe and made Amos tremble at the thunder of Yahweh's judgment, now takes on a new aspect. God is above vengeance. He will not give up his purpose of salvation, whatever its cost may be. Hosea is the most "evangelical" of the prophets — not because he takes a less radical view of the sinfulness of his people, but because he penetrates more deeply into the nature of God. There is a kinship between Hosea and John. God is love. And for both of them, to "know" God means to respond to that love. It means trust and obedience. Where there is no knowledge of God, all relationships break down, priest and prophet stumble, and "the land mourns."

Will the bitter lesson of the fate of the Northern Kingdom be a warning to the little Kingdom of Judah? Micah of Moresheth is the Amos of the south: a man of the land, who sees with scorn how the peasants have their fields and houses, their family inheritances, wrenched from them (Micah 2:2). He attacks with the utmost violence the leaders of Jerusalem and announces their doom:

> "Hear, you heads of Jacob
>   and rulers of the house of Israel!
> Is it not for you to know justice? —
>   you who hate the good and love the evil
> who tear the skin from off my people,
>   and their flesh from off their bones;
> who eat the flesh of my people,
>   and flay their skin from off them,
> and break their bones in pieces,
>   and chop them up like meat in a kettle,
> like flesh in a caldron.
>
> "Its heads give judgment for a bribe,
>   its priests teach for hire,
>   its prophets divine for money;
> yet they lean upon the Lord and say,
>   'Is not the Lord in the midst of us?
> No evil shall come upon us.'"
>   (Micah 3:1–3; 11.)

In fact, several invasions will devastate the land in Isaiah's and Micah's lifetime, and Jerusalem will know a narrow escape. In calling the powerful Assyrian Empire to the rescue against the two kingdoms of Israel and Syria, Judah had sealed its own fate. The "protector" is soon to draw a heavy tribute from the "protected." It will be Isaiah's lifelong struggle, after having vainly tried to prevent this dangerous alliance, to save Judah from getting into greater trouble by unwarranted intrigue and revolts.

Doom and Hope

The Book of Isaiah opens on a vision of God's court of justice. The Kingdom of Judah lies in the throes of war and devastation. And God calls in heaven and earth as his witnesses:

> "Hear, O heavens, and give ear, O earth;
>   for the Lord has spoken:
> 'Sons have I reared and brought up,
>   but they have rebelled against me.
> The ox knows its owner,
>   and the ass its master's crib;
> but Israel does not know,
>   my people does not understand.'"
>
> (Isa. 1:2-3.)

The judgment here again falls upon a rebellious people whose religion is divorced from life and whose hands are "full of blood." But a note of hope, a glorious promise, already rings through this great overture. If Israel repents —

> "Though your sins are like scarlet,
>   they shall be as white as snow." (Isa. 1:18.)

Never has the holiness of God Almighty been sung more powerfully than in this book; never has the note of hope alternated so rhythmically with the note of doom. Something of the majesty of God is reflected in the style of the prophet, in the calm assurance with which he dominates the events of his time. God appears to him in the glory of the Temple, "in the year that King Uzziah died" — the king struck with leprosy, whose fate must have filled his whole people with awe. Isaiah's cry: "Woe is me! For I am lost; for I am a man of unclean lips, and I dwell in the midst of a people of unclean lips; for my eyes have seen the King, the Lord of hosts!" is first of all the reaction of a sinful creature faced with the thrice holy One before whom even the seraphim cover their faces, and of whom it is said that no human being can see him and live (Isa. 6:5; see also Ex. 33:20). But is it not also the cry of a man who carries the burden of his people's uncleanness and feels himself one with king and country in their guilt?

God cleanses his lips with fire and sends him as his messenger, but with what stern warning: the people will not listen, God's word will harden their hearts! There are moments in the life of men and peoples when no power in heaven or earth can stop their downward course. They will have to touch bottom before God's word can break through. Out of this knowledge Isaiah develops the conviction that only " a remnant " can be saved.

There are two great historical scenes in Isaiah's life, one at the beginning and one at the end of his ministry. In the first, the two armies of Israel and Syria approach Jerusalem, and we are told of King Ahaz that " his heart and the heart of his people shook as the trees of the forest shake before the wind " (Isa. 7:2). The prophet alone is unshaken. The two invading armies are but "two smoldering . . . firebrands" in the sight of the King of Kings. Ahaz does not believe Isaiah (he does not want to " tempt " God! How very pious!) and he takes the fatal step of calling Assyria to the rescue. A few decades later the Assyrian army stands before Jerusalem. This time King Hezekiah believes. The Assyrian army retires during the night, much of it slain by the Lord (Isa., chs. 36; 37). The fact is confirmed by Assyrian annals, yet the cause is not clear: the decision might have been due to an epidemic or to other threats menacing Sennacherib's empire. Whatever the secondary cause, Isaiah interpreted it as the intervention of God.

Isaiah, like all the prophets of his time, sees and denounces the social unrighteousness of his day and the corruption that takes hold of the leaders of the land:

> " Woe to those who join house to house,
>   who add field to field,
>   until there is no more room,
>   and you are made to dwell alone
>   in the midst of the land." (Isa. 5:8.)

"Woe to those who rise early in the morning,
    that they may run after strong drink." (Isa. 5:11.)

He judges with special severity the women of Jerusalem, the
daughters of Zion who are "haughty" and "walk with outstretched necks, glancing wantonly with their eyes" (Isa. 3:16).

But Isaiah's main struggle remained in the political field. He
is close enough to the court to know of its intrigues; he has
fought to maintain Judah's independence. But once Judah has
become a tributary of Assyria, Isaiah sees the foolishness of all
attempts to break that yoke and to go to Egypt or Babylon for
help. It is not only foolish humanly speaking (a prophet can be
endowed by God with a good measure of human wisdom!), it
goes against the will of the Lord. Where his People are concerned, deliverance lies in his hand (see Isa., chs. 20; 30:1–5;
31:1–5).

God's Hammer

Even God's grace can become our doom. The miracle that
saved Jerusalem in Isaiah's time will soon be interpreted as a
proof that Zion is impregnable. Is it not the City of David on
which God's promises rest? Has it not God's Temple within its
walls? This is the false religious security that the mighty hammer of God's Word is now going to break to pieces. It will be
Jeremiah's task to uncover the fallacies by which leaders and
people support dangerous hopes.

His most direct attack is against the abuses of the Temple.
The old fight against a religion divorced from life goes on.
"Thus says the Lord of hosts, the God of Israel, Amend your
ways and your doings, and I will let you dwell in this place. Do
not trust in these deceptive words: 'This is the temple of the
Lord, the temple of the Lord, the temple of the Lord.' . . . Has
this house, which is called by my name, become a den of robbers
in your eyes?" (Jer. 7:3–4, 11.)

Jeremiah's first discourses are a passionate pleading with the

96 THE WITNESSING COMMUNITY

unfaithful bride, Jerusalem, to return to her lover, the God of
Israel. When no repentance occurs, the message of Jeremiah
becomes one of doom, of impending disaster. He will live to
see his darkest prophecies fulfilled, king and people dragged
into exile, Jerusalem and the Temple destroyed. Never has the
solitude of a prophet been described in more poignant terms.
This tender man whose heart hungers for human love will have
to stand alone all his life, rejected by his own people of Ana-
thoth, by the priests of Jerusalem, by prophets and kings. God's
commandment is relentless: " Behold, I make you this day a
fortified city, an iron pillar, and bronze walls, against the whole
land." (Jer. 1:18.)

Jeremiah tells about his anguish of soul, his temptation to run
away from duty. He complains that he has " become a laughing-
stock all the day " (Jer. 20:7)! But God does not let him go:

> " If I say, ' I will not mention him,
>   or speak any more in his name,'
> there is in my heart as it were a burning fire
>   shut up in my bones,
> and I am weary with holding it in,
>   and I cannot."
>   (Jer. 20:9; see also chs. 11; 12; 15:10-21.)

Here again the prophetic message is directed first of all
against the leaders of Judah: they have been entrusted with specific functions as king, as magistrate, as priest or prophet. It is
the betrayal of these functions that is their greatest sin in the
sight of God, because every authority comes from him and is
answerable to him. Therefore, woe to the king who lets his people be exploited and killed! Woe to the judge who can be
bought for money! Woe to the priest who conforms to the trend
of the times! Woe to the prophet who tells lies!

Not all kings or priests are bad. In Isaiah's time King Hezekiah had attempted a reform. But his work had been destroyed
by Manasseh, who went so far as to allow child slaughter and

to introduce sacred prostitution in the Temple of Jerusalem. Of his grandson, Josiah, it is said that " he did what was right in the eyes of the Lord, and walked in all the way of David his father, and he did not turn aside to the right hand or to the left " (II Kings 22:2). A book is brought to the king by order of the high priest — a proof that also among the priesthood there are those who preserve the true Yahwistic tradition! Presumably it was Deuteronomy. "And when the king heard the words of the book of the law, he rent his clothes." (II Kings 22:11.) Orders are given to destroy the high places and remove the idols from the land; the Temple is purified and the cult prostitutes are suppressed. Why does The Book of Jeremiah refer only briefly to this drastic reform (see Jer. 11:1–8)? Maybe the prophet soon lost all hope for its effectiveness. Maybe it was too legalistic. It did not bring about the required circumcision of the " heart " (Jer. 4:4; see also Deut. 30:6). It was too late. Jehoiakim, Josiah's son, in a memorable scene not long after, tore Jeremiah's scrolls to pieces (see Jer., ch. 36).

See how sarcastic Jeremiah can be as he utters God's judgments on Jehoiakim:

> " 'Woe to him who builds his house by unrighteousness,
>   and his upper rooms by injustice;
> who makes his neighbor serve him for nothing,
>   and does not give him his wages;
> who says, "I will build myself a great house
>   with spacious upper rooms,"
> and cuts out windows for it,
>   paneling it with cedar,
>   and painting it with vermilion.
> Do you think you are a king
>   because you compete in cedar?
> Did not your father eat and drink
>   and do justice and righteousness?
>   Then it was well with him.
> He judged the cause of the poor and needy;
>   then it was well.

Is not this to know me?
   says the Lord.
But you have eyes and heart
   only for your dishonest gain,
for shedding innocent blood,
   and for practicing oppression and violence.'
Therefore thus says the Lord . . . :
   'They shall not lament for him, saying,
   "Ah lord!" or "Ah his majesty!"
With the burial of an ass he shall be buried,
   dragged and cast forth beyond the gates of Jerusalem.'"
(Jer. 22:13-19.)

The weak King Zedekiah, Jehoiakim's successor, put on the throne by Nebuchadrezzar, will have more pious regard for the prophet: "Pray for us to the Lord" (Jer. 37:3). But he will not have the courage to listen to him! And Jeremiah's indignation will burst out once more when king and prince, after proclaiming liberty for the slaves by solemn oath during the siege of Jerusalem, take back their promise as soon as the siege is over (see Jer., ch. 34). How often similar promises have been made to subject peoples in times of war and taken back in times of peace! But the price of unrighteousness has to be paid sooner or later.

The first deportation took to Babylon the elite of Jerusalem. Those who remain like to think of themselves as the good people whom God protects. Here again the prophet's word goes counter to public opinion: the " good figs " are the departed, the bad figs remain! It is now in Babylon and no more in Jerusalem that God will build up the faithful remnant! Israel will be deprived for a time of all the tokens of God's covenant: the Promised Land, the Davidic dynasty, the Temple. It will have to learn that God is not bound to a place: his glory will shine above the distant River Chebar. And among the exiles, a new watchman will be called to stand over Israel: the prophet Ezekiel (see Ezek. 1:1-3; 3:12-21; 33:7).

God's Word Makes Free Men

What guidance can we find in the prophetic message for the present day?

For several centuries the prophets were the channel of God's revelation to his People. When the Fulfiller came, prophecy, in the Old Testament meaning of the word, ended. Yet there is a prophetic function of the church: it must proclaim God's Word and interpret it to every generation. The problem of the preacher is whether he will listen to that Word until it takes possession of him so that he too will be, not a man "dreaming dreams" or speaking out of his own wisdom, but the "mouth of God" — the channel through which the Spirit does his witnessing work. Then, and then only, will he be a true watchman in church and city.

To stand under God means to see all things in his light. The Word, earnestly listened to, makes *free men,* able to look at themselves and at the world in all fairness and independence of mind. This is the great lesson that we all have constantly to relearn. And this freedom under God should not be the attribute of the preacher only, but of all church members. There must be a corporate as well as a personal "standing under God's word" if we are to interpret his will for our own time. It is a task that requires ever-renewed searching of heart. The contemporary world, so full of slogans and catchwords, needs nothing so much as to hear the voice of such free men. Their insights are needed in all walks of life, in education as well as in industry and politics. If the church does not provide them, who will?

We have seen all through this chapter that one of the prophets' main attacks is directed against the divorce of religion from everyday life. Religion is not a kind of life insurance for the future, nor a soothing panacea amidst the troubles of this world. What the God of Israel requires is total commitment of the whole life. "You shall have no other gods before me"! The prophets are relentless destroyers of idols, and idols are not only

Asherah or Tammuz — they include the Temple, the state, power, money, and success: Man deified.

We have also seen how seriously the prophets take professional responsibility. The place where we live and work is the real place where our obedience toward God must find its most concrete expression.

And finally, all through, there is a tremendous concern for justice. In the prophetic writings as in the law of Israel, God is the defender of the defenseless. God stands with the underdog! Is not this one of the points where the church has failed? How weak during the nineteenth century was the church's defense of the exploited workers! In Europe, as a consequence, it has lost the world of labor. Is not the rise of communism God's judgment on the compliance of the church with the wealthy and powerful of this world? Has not the church all too long tolerated the current policies in matters of race and of subject peoples? Has it not often been more vigorous in its defense of the rights of property than in the protection of human lives?

Today, of course, the church awakens to these problems; but so does the secular world! Shall we always deal with yesterday's problems rather than tomorrow's?

The fight of the prophets was against institutionalism and organization as substitutes for real personal life. And yet, how elementary were Israel's institutions as compared with ours! The techniques of industry and trade, of government and diplomacy, were in their infancy; but already man asserted his autonomy in all fields, and the great empires seemed impressive statues of iron, silver, and gold — but with feet of clay. The twentieth century is the age of technology. And technology has its positive sides. It has raised the standards of living of millions of people in the West, and similar developments seem to be the only way to save Asia from disease, drought, and starvation. A Christian should acknowledge all this.

At the same time, he should see where the present trend is

leading us. As our society becomes more and more highly organized, the person tends to be seen and valued in terms of his
usefulness to society as a whole; he is a cog or a wheel in the
big machine. Natural entities — the family, the village — lose
their organic, corporate existence and are swallowed up in the
gregarious anonymity of city life. The welfare state sees each
person as "a case" to be treated according to well-defined
techniques. It takes in hand both youth and old age.

On the whole, personal relationships are sacrificed to the
interests (or supposed interests) of the masses. An extreme example of this is the communist regimes, in which the whole life
of the state is keyed to production and the present generation is
deliberately sacrificed to future achievements. It is unquestion-
able that this can mean, in the long run, higher standards of
living for the destitute masses of such countries as Russia or
China. What remains to be seen is what kind of human being
will emerge from the experiment.

But this overly materialistic view of life should not hide from
our eyes that a similar danger is threatening the West in spite
of all the "religion" it still professes. In a shrewd analysis of
present trends in his book *Protestant, Catholic, Jew* (Double-
day & Co., Inc., 1955), Prof. Will Herberg shows that the
real god of many Americans today is "the American way of
life" — efficiency, success. A very subtle idol clad in garments
of light! In fact, the trend is a powerful one, not only in America but, to different degrees and in different forms, all over the
world.

A recent French book by Jacques Ellul, professor of law in
Bordeaux (*La technique ou l'enjeu du siècle*, Paris, Armand
Colin, 1954), taking "technique" (in a wider sense than that
commonly used in the English language) to mean a certain
mode of organization, shows how "techniques" tend to dominate all realms of life by a kind of irresistible self-propulsion.
The technical age began with the invention of the machine;

but the machine called for a new technique of production, a new technique of salesmanship, of international trade and finances. Needs and problems developed on such a scale that state control became necessary in order to preserve the common interests of the citizens. A new technique of government evolved, carrying in its wings a skillful technique of propaganda. We have learned not only how to handle things, but how to handle men and groups. The techniques of psychology and sociology, of group work, help us to build a "happy community" where frictions will be avoided. Preventive measures are taken to eliminate the troublesome elements by discreet police control. State education trains children to fit into the common pattern of life. The great art is to help people "adjust" to their environments, so that the machine of society can run smoothly.

This all runs beautifully, except that in such a society human beings tend to become cogs in the machine, carefully oiled to avoid friction! For example, the workers are treated a hundred times better than a century ago. But the change has come about not so much because we are more sensitive to their welfare as human beings as for two other obvious reasons: first, that well-treated workers produce more and better; and secondly, that trade unions have developed a high technique of self-defense. We should be glad for the result but sober as to its causes. Where these two factors are not present — in underdeveloped countries, for instance — human exploitation has gone on to this day.

In another recent book (*The Lonely Crowd*) an American sociologist shows that mankind goes through three great stages: what he calls the "tradition directed" (tribal system), the "inner directed," and the "other directed" period. The inner directed period comes when opportunities are great and initiative is needed — as in the frontier period. Other-directedness comes when a given society is saturated and "adjustment" becomes a condition of survival. According to the author, our Western civilization is in process of reaching this third stage. While any classification of this kind runs the danger of oversimplification, we believe this one contains an element of truth and this truth is alarming. The call to conform is not the monopoly of dictatorships.

Who will resist this trend to conformity? The university? It has done so sometimes; we have seen this happen in Holland during the occupation. The University of Leyden chose to be closed rather than to allow the Jews to be excluded. We have had recent examples of it in the United States. On the whole it must be said that intellectuals have all too often kept silent and adapted their thinking to the trends of the day.

Who then will stand firm, if not the Christian church? Here again we have had startling examples of resistance: the Confessing Church in Germany, a man like Bishop Berggrav in Norway. Such have been, in times of crisis, the watchmen standing over the city, whatever be the cost. There is one category of men the authors of *The Lonely Crowd* do not seem to know: those who are other-directed, not by man but *by God;* the nonconformist prophets of all times. But here again we must listen to the prophets of old: their fight was a lonely one and so may ours be.

In the realm of religion, conformity does not necessarily take crude forms, especially in a nation that still holds to traditional Christianity. It can mean a refined kind of syncretism that we like to call " broad-mindedness ": all faiths are equal, provided they make good people. It can mean a subtle process of secularization by which the methods and standards of church and world become so very much the same that the message of the church is quite innocuous — and very welcome. " All is well, all is well! " It can mean that religion becomes itself a valued asset in the state machinery: it provides spiritual security and " peace of mind " to an otherwise restless generation.

God's Word is a hammer which smashes the rock to pieces.

God's Word is a consuming fire. God's Word is a two-edged sword which cuts the hand that holds it.

This is the prophets' hard answer to our human demand for earthly and religious securities.

CHAPTER VII

The Prophetic View of History

" For behold, I create new heavens and a new earth;
and the former things shall not be remembered."
(Isa. 65:17.)

The prophetic conception of history could be summarized in two sentences: God is Lord of history. Therefore, history has meaning; it leads somewhere.

There is a crucial problem for modern man. One of the causes of pessimism and despair in present-day Europe is that many are overcome by the feeling of the *meaninglessness of history*. History seems to be cyclic. Civilizations grow, bloom, and disappear. We have probably attained the high point of our so-called Western culture, and there are already clear signs of decay. One of the main reasons for the success of Marxism is that Marxism has a theory of history that promises people a future, something definite to strive for, a definite means of attaining the goal. This explains the optimistic mood of communist countries, at least in the early stages of their development. The future belongs to them! On the other hand, many of our democracies seem to have lost the strong drive that leads people to daring action: they do not see clearly their vocation in history. This is a serious political problem, but it has deeper roots. The underlying faith is lacking, the belief that history has meaning and a goal.

It was the acuteness of the problem of history that led the World Council of Churches to center its studies, at the time of the Evanston Assembly, on the *Christian hope*. But these studies have shown how difficult it is really to grip the hearts and minds of people with a theme of this kind. Why? Is it because this hope sounds too otherworldly? Or is it because we have ceased to believe in God as the actual Lord of history, of our own as well as of world history?

God Is Lord

The prophets did believe in God as the Lord of history. How did they come to this conviction? What concrete results did this conviction have for their interpretation of their own times? What was their people's place in this history? How did they see the goal of all history, and how was God's ultimate victory to be won? These are some of the questions we would like to examine in this chapter.

First, we have already seen that God reveals himself to the prophet as an actual power at work in the life of his people. God speaks and the thing is. The personal encounter is the starting point of the witness. Secondly, God opens the eyes of the prophet so that he sees the world as it is, or, in other words, as God sees it. The secret motives of men are uncovered, the deadly forces at work in the world are called by name. Thirdly, the prophet knows about God's covenant with his People. His promises hold. The ultimate victory belongs to Him. Judgment is never God's sole and last word. An unbreakable hope runs through the prophetic message. Its form may change, but never its ultimate certainty. For this certainty is based on the very nature of God. "The gifts and the call of God are irrevocable." (Rom. 11:29.) He will achieve his saving purpose, he will remain true to himself and fulfill his Word, by means known to him alone.

The great prophets of the eighth and seventh centuries B.C. have a very concrete view of God's action in history. They "see" his hand on his chosen People, calling, delivering, judging, redeeming. It is he who sends rain and drought, locusts and earthquake. Foreign armies hurry at his summons from the ends of the earth, their arrows sharp, their bows bent, to chastise his unfaithful people (see Isa. 5:26–30; 10:5–6).

It is precisely at this point that difficulties begin for the modern reader. He knows about the complexities of nature and history; he cannot relate all events to a single transcendent cause. Moreover, a Christian will be reluctant to ascribe to God's will all the catastrophes of history.

On this point we have a precious saying of Jesus himself which can guide us in our interpretation of the prophetic message. When the disciples question him on the matter of the Galileans massacred by Pilate, Jesus answers: "Do you think that these Galileans were worse sinners than all the other Galileans, because they suffered thus? I tell you, No; but unless you repent you will all likewise perish " (Luke 13:2). Every crisis in history is seen here as a call to repentance, a warning. This is the real and permanent meaning of the prophetic message. In the words of Hosea, those who "sow the wind . . . shall reap the whirlwind " (Hos. 8:7). What the message of the prophets implies is that there are certain God-given laws of life that cannot be broken except by nations running toward destruction.

The first and perhaps the greatest exponent of God's sovereign rule over *all* history is Amos. As over against those who would consider God's rule as limited to Israel, Amos stresses the fact that all nations stand under God. "Did I not bring up Israel from the land of Egypt, and the Philistines from Caphtor and the Syrians from Kir?" (Amos 9:7.) This is a new and striking statement. It seems to put Israel on the same level as other nations. *All* are standing under God's mercy and judgment. But they are judged according to the degree of knowledge granted to them. Amos hears God roar like a lion against Damascus and Gaza, against Tyre and Edom, against Ammon and Moab, because they have transgressed elementary rules of behavior that all these people held in common. There are certain laws of warfare, of justice and mercy, that should be respected by all human beings. They have threshed the enemy with "threshing sledges of iron" (Amos 1:3); they have deported a whole people and delivered them to their foes; they have desecrated the dead king; they have broken the covenant with the sister tribe; they have "cast off all pity" (Amos 1:11). These indictments of Amos are very important. They show that the Bible acknowledges a certain elementary law of right and wrong, written in the hearts of men, for the breaking of which they are answerable to the holy God. Paul acknowledges this law "written on their hearts" according to which the Gentiles will be judged at the Last Judgment (see Rom. 2:14-15).

We may suppose that the Israelites listened with a certain glee to these poems in which all their hated neighbors stood accused in God's court. A preacher who, in times of war, thunders against the enemy is pretty sure of approval, even in our day. But how unexpected the conclusion: "Your crime is the worst! Because you know better!"

> "You only have I known
>   of all the families of the earth;
> *therefore* I will punish you
>   for all your iniquities."
>   (Amos 3:2.)

Election implies that we stand in a unique way under God's judgment, not that we escape judgment. Purging and sifting begin with the chosen People, with the church. Those who have received more will be treated more severely. To belong to God's People is not a haven of security. Both Amos and Jeremiah had a hard time breaking through the nation's false sense of security! Israel cannot help seeing the Lord's Day as the day of its own triumph.

> "Woe to you who desire the day of the Lord!
>   Why would you have the day of the Lord?
> It is darkness, and not light."
>   (Amos 5:18.)

The catastrophes of history are seen by the prophets as a fore-taste of the Last Judgment. They disclose the power of the forces of evil suddenly let loose. They dispel all our false man-made securities. They show that God is not mocked and that his hand lies on history. In this deep sense, they must be received as a judgment of God on mankind's foolish ways.

It is indeed a mysterious choice of God's providence that placed the Promised Land at the most exposed spot in the ancient world, on the highways that led from the northern and eastern great powers to Egypt and Arabia. Palestine is a pre-destined battlefield, like the Low Countries in Europe. It could not, in the long run, escape being taken into the whirlwind of world politics. The United Kingdom of Israel was built up at a time when both Egypt and the Asian empires had weakened, but this was only a short respite. In the space of a few centuries, Palestine was to be subjected to Assyria, Egypt, Babylon, Persia, Greece, and Rome. Later it fell a prey to the Moslem power. And how precarious its independence seems again today! The chosen People of God cannot escape the impact of the world which surrounds them. Maybe this is a condition of their world mission.

" By the Strength of My Hand "

The prophets see the invasion of Assyria and later of Babylon as a chastisement of God — God's " rod." They do not hesitate to call Nebuchadrezzar God's " servant," as they will later call Cyrus God's " anointed." But the foreign nations ignore the fact that their power comes from God. Therefore, this power soon becomes demonic. How shrewdly the prophets have ana-lyzed this vertigo of self-assertion which leads to the heights of power and ends in the abyss!

" When the Lord has finished all his work on Mount Zion and on Jerusalem he will punish the arrogant boasting of the king of Assyria and his haughty pride. For he says:

> " ' By the strength of my hand I have done it,
>   and by my wisdom, for I have understanding.' . . .
> " Shall the ax vaunt itself over him who hews with it,
>   or the saw magnify itself against him who wields it?
> As if a rod should wield him who lifts it,
>   or as if a staff should lift him who is not wood! "
>   (Isa. 10:12–13, 15.)

" By the strength of my hand I have done it "! Is not this the
recurrent temptation of all earthly success for both individuals
and nations? And this self-glorification is nothing but the old
Promethean dream, nothing but the fundamental longing of
natural man to make himself into a god. With what powerful
irony the prophets break the idol! " Thus says the Lord God:

> " ' Behold, I am against you,
>   Pharaoh king of Egypt,
> the great dragon that lies
>   in the midst of his streams,
> that says, " My Nile is my own;
>   I made it."
> I will put hooks in your jaws,
>   and make the fish of your streams stick to your scales;
> and I will draw you up out of the midst of your streams,
>   with all the fish of your streams
>   which stick to your scales.
> And I will cast you forth into the wilderness,
>   you and all the fish of your streams.' " (Ezek. 29:3–5.)

How beautifully the same prophet describes the beauty and
the wealth of Tyre, the queen of the seas! But here again the
vertigo of power seizes the city:

> " You have said, ' I am a god,
> I sit in the seat of the gods,
>   in the heart of the seas.' . . .
> Will you still say, ' I am a god,'
>   in the presence of those who slay you? "
>   (Ezek. 28:2, 9.)

Indeed, the city was a " signet of perfection, full of wisdom and perfect in beauty " (Ezek. 28:12)! But:

> " In the abundance of your trade
> you were filled with violence, and you sinned." (V. 16.)

Tyre is condemned not for her beauty, her wealth, her culture, but for her self-deification and for the will-to-power ending in cruelty and greed.

Have not the prophets given us here a deep insight into world history? Nationalism runs high in our time. We have seen empires rise and fall. Dictators have made themselves into little gods. How strangely the prophet's funeral song over the king of Babylon rings in our ears:

> " Sheol beneath is stirred up
>   to meet you when you come,
>   it rouses the shades to greet you,
>   all who were leaders of the earth;
>   it raises from their thrones
>   all who were kings of the nations.
> All of them will speak
>   and say to you:
> ' You too have become as weak as we!
>   You have become like us! ' . . .
> " How you are fallen from heaven,
>   O Day Star, son of Dawn!
> How you are cut down to the ground,
>   you who laid the nations low! . . .
> Those who see you will stare at you,
>   and ponder over you:
> ' Is this the man who made the earth tremble,
>   who shook kingdoms,
> who made the world like a desert
>   and overthrew its cities,
>   who did not let his prisoners go home? ' "
>   (Isa. 14:9–10, 12, 16–17.)

Never, in all literature, has the vanity of earthly power been described more forcefully. Lust for power breeds its own reward, even in this world. But if the ruthless ruler should escape judgment on earth, there is a Last Judgment which awaits him.

This insight into the vanity of power built on sheer force is one of the reasons for the prophet's stand against Israel's diplomatic intrigues. Egypt will prove to be but " a broken reed " to those who lean on it! But there is a deeper motive for the prophet's warning. Israel has only one sure defender: God, the Lord. Where God fights for his People, no power can overcome them. This is Isaiah's stand. Where God condemns them, nothing can save them. This will be the basis of Jeremiah's so-called " defeatist " attitude.

How far can we follow the prophets' lead on this point? Israel, as God's People, had a unique destiny; it was not " like all the nations," but a theocracy under God. Church and state were one. Therefore, some discrimination is needed when we are tempted to apply to a modern state what was said to Israel. But it is the church's prophetic function to remind the state — all states — that no lasting power can be built on sheer force. Our Lord himself has warned us that he who draws the sword will perish by the sword. We live in a time of judgment when colonial powers pay the price of past exploitation and greed. Other and more severe judgments may be ahead. This must be seen and said. The church, at least, should take seriously the prophet's warning:

> " Woe to those who go down to Egypt for help
> and rely on horses,
> who trust in chariots because they are many
> and in horsemen because they are very strong,
> but do not look to the Holy One of Israel
> or consult the Lord! . . .
> The Egyptians are men, and not God;
> and their horses are flesh, and not spirit.
> When the Lord stretches out his hand,
> the helper will stumble, and he who is helped will fall,
> and they will all perish together."   (Isa. 31:1, 3.)

A Gate of Hope

Judgment holds a great place in the prophetic utterance. We have seen that it is the very calling of the prophet to stand as a watchman over the city when the appointed rulers forsake their duties. But judgment is never God's sole and last word: his work in history is a work of salvation. This is the other aspect of the prophet's message.

Israel will be chastened and sifted; but it remains God's chosen instrument for the salvation of the world. God will not leave himself without witnesses: a *remnant* will survive and a time will come when Israel will be a blessing to all families on earth; a time when even Egypt and Assyria will be "healed," when "there will be a highway from Egypt to Assyria, and the Assyrian will come into Egypt, and the Egyptian into Assyria. . . . In that day Israel will be the third with Egypt and Assyria, a blessing in the midst of the earth, whom the Lord of hosts has blessed, saying, 'Blessed be Egypt my people, and Assyria the work of my hands, and Israel my heritage.'" This is perhaps the greatest ecumenical vision of the Old Testament!

Even The Book of Amos, in which the note of doom is so predominant, ends with a promise of restoration. Whether or not this is due to a later hand does not alter the theological significance of the fact. A given prophet at a given time may be called to strike one single note; but the total prophetic message is one of *both* judgment and hope. It is a striking fact that the prophets come out with an outright word of doom when all others around them feel secure. They cry, "Judgment!" when others are saying: "All is well! All is well! Trade is booming, the standards of living are high. Why worry?" But when the judgment has taken place, when shallow optimism has been replaced by black despair, the prophet is the one who will give the note of hope. Jeremiah, a prisoner in a besieged city, buys a field as a token of oncoming deliverance. Ezekiel is given the vision of dead bones coming to life. This is the prophet's insight:

he sees the worm at the heart of the tree when fruit and foliage still look healthy to the undiscerning eye. He sees the hidden seed secretly sown by God even when the earth looks void and desolate.

The question might well be asked whether the church has the same prophetic discernment. Do we not all too often follow, rather than precede, the tide of the time? Did we not indulge, at the turn of the century, in a doctrine of progress and success? And now that the self-confidence of men and nations is seriously shaken, are we ready to proclaim the hope that no earthly turmoil can destroy — the power of Christ's resurrection and the power of the Spirit to build life out of chaos?

How, according to the prophets, is salvation to take place? Certainly by an act of God, not by human endeavor. But it will take place within history. The vision of the early prophets is that of a Kingdom that will renew and outgrow the splendor of David's reign. A child will be born on whom all dominion will rest. The nations shall flow to Zion to be instructed in the ways of the Lord (see Isa. 2:1–4; 9:1–7). Yet, even in these early visions our earthly condition is suddenly transcended: we are lifted beyond the realm of history; the broken unity between God and his creation is restored. Not only does righteousness prevail, but even the animal world will enjoy God's peace:

> " The wolf shall dwell with the lamb,
>   and the leopard shall lie down with the kid."
>   (See Isa. 11:1–9.)

" New Heavens and a New Earth "

The prophets' paradise is no spiritual, abstract condition, but rather a transformed earth, bursting with the joys of life. The exiles will hear again " the voice of mirth and the voice of gladness, the voice of the bridegroom and the voice of the bride, the voices of those who sing, as they bring thank offerings to the house of the Lord " (Jer. 33:11). Sufferings will be forgotten:

" For behold, I create new heavens
   and a new earth;
and the former things shall not be remembered
   or come into mind.
But be glad and rejoice for ever
   in that which I create;
for behold, I create Jerusalem a rejoicing,
   and her people a joy. . . .
They shall build houses and inhabit them;
   they shall plant vineyards and eat their fruit.
They shall not build and another inhabit;
   they shall not plant and another eat;
for like the days of a tree shall the days of my people be,
   and my chosen shall long enjoy the work of their hands."
                                        (Isa. 65:17-18, 21-22.)

All the suffering of the poor and the exploited finds its expression in such verses. The nearest to it outside the Bible is perhaps the faith expressed in some old Negro spirituals. Shall we
call such expectations materialistic? Are they not rather the
concrete expression of that hunger and thirst for justice so typi-
cal of Israel's faith? There must be fullness of life for all. And
this in our limited human language can only be expressed in
material images. But the essence of this new life is that

" The earth shall be full of the knowledge of the Lord
   as the waters cover the sea." (Isa. 11:9; see also Hab. 2:14.)

Skeptical minds will immediately raise a question: Have not
all times been dreaming of a golden age? How can it be proved
that this is not " pious wishing "? The certainty of the prophet
is based on his knowledge of God as the living God. This is
what differentiates the prophet from the dreamer. By his whole
history, the faithful Israelite knows of God's saving power and
steadfastness of purpose. Only he who is committed to God's
Word can testify that *it works*. Where there is in our Christian
life no living relation with the risen Christ, no reliance on the
power of the Spirit, our hope will be dim and easily shaken by

outward circumstances. The prophet's vision is the vision of faith. He can no more doubt God's ultimate victory than he can doubt his existence.

In this perspective, every deliverance contains something of the reality of the ultimate deliverance, as every judgment contains something of the reality of the Last Judgment. Thus the conquest of the Promised Land had been a token of the Kingdom to come. The restoration following the Babylonian deportation was very different from the exiles' expectations. How humble the painfully constructed Temple, how poor the devastated city! Nevertheless, they were a sign of God's mercy, a promise of a greater deliverance yet to come. And slowly the faithful Jewish remnant began to understand that such a deliverance could not come through the building up of an earthly kingdom, but only by God's intervention from above. This became the meaning of Jewish apocalyptic, of Daniel's vision of the Son of Man coming with the clouds of heaven. (For the importance of the expression " Son of Man " and its use by Jesus, see Theo Preiss, " Le Fils de l'Homme," *Études Théologique et Religieuses,* Montpellier. Part I, 1951; Part II, 1953).

The Clue to History

Yet, the clue to world history is ultimately to be found neither in the Messianic Kingdom visualized by the prophets, nor in the apocalyptic expectations of a later age, although both of these express an essential part of the truth of God's Kingship over his creation and the transcendental nature of its manifestation. The decisive answer to the riddle of history is given in Deutero-Isaiah, in the mysterious figure of the *Ebed Yahweh,* the Servant of God.

In a series of songs, the Servant is pictured to us as the One in whom God finds his delight, the One on whom God's Spirit rests. What characterizes him is not power but humility, unfailing justice, capacity to endure suffering and utter rejection. He will be despised and abhorred by the nations, and yet the day will come when kings and princes will prostrate themselves before him. He will be a light to the nations and bring God's salvation to the end of the earth. And yet, at the time of his appearance, who will believe in him?

> "He had no form or comeliness that we should look at him,
>   and no beauty that we should desire him.
> He was despised and rejected by men;
>   a man of sorrows, and acquainted with grief;
> and as one from whom men hide their faces
>   he was despised, and we esteemed him not.
> "Surely he has borne our griefs
>   and carried our sorrows;
> yet we esteemed him stricken,
>   smitten by God, and afflicted.
> But he was wounded for our transgressions,
>   he was bruised for our iniquities;
> upon him was the chastisement that made us whole,
>   and with his stripes we are healed."

(Isa. 53:2-5.)

Who is this servant? A prophet? The faithful remnant? The expected Messiah? Jewish exegesis has generally seen in this figure the chosen People, rejected by the nations, set apart by God for his service, carrying by the very fact of their unique vocation the weight of human guilt. The Christian church has unhesitatingly recognized in this prophecy a portrait of its Lord. Who else could atone for the sins of the world? The Gospels show that Jesus himself accepted as his way the way of the Suffering Servant, and that way as over against all glorious expectations.

Yet it should be stressed that the two interpretations do not necessarily exclude one another: for the Christian, Jesus *is* the true Israel: in him is the vocation of the chosen People fulfilled. He is God's true witness. He offers himself for the salvation of the nations. At the same time, God's People bear the marks of their election in Christ. The destiny of Israel is one of suffering, of testimony unto blood. The last word of the prophets' "philosophy of history" is this tremendous affirmation that the powers of evil can only be met and conquered, ultimately, by the power of vicarious suffering. "Not by might, nor by power, but by my Spirit, says the Lord of hosts." (Zech. 4:6.)

The church's one hope in history, and beyond history, lies in the victory of the crucified and risen Lord. The only power by which it can ultimately overcome the ideologies and lusts of the nations is the power of the cross. Only for those who know Christ and the power of his resurrection and the fellowship of his sufferings has history — their own history or world history — any ultimate meaning.

CHAPTER VIII

Frustration and Hope: The Remnant

> *" Though the fig tree do not blossom,*
> *nor fruit be on the vines,*
> *the produce of the olive fail*
> *and the fields yield no food,*
> *the flock be cut off from the fold*
> *and there be no herd in the stalls,*
> *yet I will rejoice in the Lord,*
> *I will joy in the God of my salvation."*
> (Hab. 3:17–18.)

The Babylonian exile was to bring about certain fundamental changes in the religious life of Israel. The People of God ceased, except for a brief period, to exist as an independent state, as a " nation "; they were reduced to a " remnant " and at the same time became more definitely a religious community. The necessity of carrying on the faith even when deprived of Temple worship led the Jews of the Dispersion to a reappraisal of their tradition, and to a new stress on the law and on such institutions as the Sabbath. This is probably the origin of a new form of worship, centering more on the Word. Thus arose the cult of the synagogue, which we find widespread all through the Jewish Dispersion a few centuries later. This does not mean that the Temple lost its importance. It remained the God-given center of worship, an object of longing, of reverence and love, without which Israel's faith would have been incomplete. But at the same time Judaism was to become more and more the religion of the

Book, nourished by the Word. A great literary activity seems to have started during the exile. Priestly circles collected ancient sources and put them into final shape. One of the main works to come out of this was the " Torah " — the first five books of the Bible. (" Torah " means the revelation of God's will for his People — his law manifested in word and deed.)

The Nation Becomes a Religious Community.

Looking back, we may wonder why God allowed Israel so long to identify its religious with its national life, risking all the dangers such an identification implies. We should see that this was a necessary development at a time when the individual's life and faith could not be detached from the corporate existence of the tribe or nation. Israel had to have a " living space," a place on earth where God's sovereignty could find a concrete expression in terms both of worship and of social life. God led his People to Palestine at the very moment when world history made a relatively autonomous existence of that little people possible for a few centuries. God further prepared a nucleus of believers (here both Deuteronomy and the prophetic message had an important role to play) who not only survived the turmoil of war and destruction, but were able to draw the lesson from these events and to prepare the ground for a deeper personal faith.

The Babylonian exile was not, humanly speaking, an altogether unhappy experience. Many Jews settled in Babylon, becoming expert merchants and bankers, and the Jewish colony there was to remain for centuries to come an influential center of Jewry, while similar colonies began to flourish in Egypt. For those Jews, a return to an impoverished Palestine offered no inviting prospects; most of them stayed. Those who returned were probably the poorer elements of the population. They were helped in their endeavor by goods and money from the rich who had found a new home abroad. (There is a strange similarity between what happened then and what happens today in the modern State of Israel.)

For the pious elements of the population, Jerusalem remained an object of passionate love:

> " By the waters of Babylon,
> there we sat down and wept,
> when we remembered Zion.
> On the willows there
> we hung up our lyres.
> For there our captors
> required of us songs,
> and our tormentors, mirth, saying,
> ' Sing us one of the songs of Zion! '
> " How shall we sing the Lord's song
> in a foreign land?
> If I forget you, O Jerusalem,
> let my right hand wither!
> Let my tongue cleave to the roof
> of my mouth,
> if I do not remember you,
> if I do not set Jerusalem
> above my highest joy! "
>
> (Ps. 137:1-6.)

Is this the deep longing of the exile for the homeland — this nagging sickness which lies hidden in the heart of so many refugees when recalling the hills and fields, the songs and perfumes, all the things that entered from infancy into the very texture of their souls? It is all this, and yet much more. For Jerusalem is no ordinary city. It is God's holy hill; it is the place where " the tribes of the Lord " assembled in joyful throngs:

> "I was glad when they said to me,
> ' Let us go to the house of the Lord! '
> Our feet have been standing
> within your gates, O Jerusalem! "
>
> (Ps. 122:1-2.)

Now Jerusalem is a forlorn city:

> "She weeps bitterly in the night, . . .
> "Her gates have sunk into the ground;
>   he [the Lord] has ruined and broken her bars;
> her king and princes are among the nations;
>   the law is no more
> and her prophets obtain
>   no vision from the Lord." (Lam. 1:2; 2:9.)

We must grasp the depth of this grief and this sense of a frustrated vocation if we are to understand the present struggle in the Near East. What other people in the history of the world has survived its national existence for nineteen centuries and still maintained its inner cohesion, its expectations? We ourselves have seen the place where the Temple once stood and where the beautiful Mosque of Omar now stands, having stood there more centuries than did all three Temples of Yahweh. And nearby, we saw an old man and a young woman, kissing the stones of the Wall of Lamentations: the faithful Israel mourning for its lost city and waiting still for its restoration! The problem that awaited the returning exiles in 538 B.C.— about 2,500 years ago!—has not changed much either. New settlers had occupied most of the land. This had already happened in Samaria under Assyrian control, bringing all the religious syncretism which that involved (see II Kings 17:24-34; Ezra 4:1-3).

After the Babylonian victory, many towns in Judah had been razed and the territory, greatly reduced, was considered as a mere district under the control of the governors of Samaria. Arab, Edomite, and Ammonite raiders constantly threatened the dismantled city of Jerusalem, as can be seen in Nehemiah's account of the situation around 445 B.C.

No wonder that, for the century that followed Cyrus' edict allowing the Jews to return and to rebuild their Temple, the tiny Jewish community in Jerusalem remained very weak. It was about twenty years before the Temple was rebuilt, and it needed Haggai's and Zechariah's ardent pleading to set the people to work. How vivid, to anyone who has lived through a postwar period in a devastated land, sound the prophet's words: "You have sown much, and harvested little; you eat, but you never have enough; you drink, but you never have your fill; you clothe yourselves, but no one is warm; and he who earns wages earns wages to put them into a bag with holes"! (Hag. 1:6.) To the prophet all this misery comes because the people have constructed "paneled houses" for themselves while leaving the Lord's house in ruins (Hag. 1:4).

Is not the right to worship their God as ordered the main aim of the restoration? While Zechariah's prophecies show clearly that the returned exiles looked for a time to Zerubbabel and Joshua as the temporal and the spiritual leaders of the new community, the former soon vanishes from the picture and the stress henceforth is on the religious community. Israel is a "hierocracy," under the authority of the high priest.

But even a religious community needs a minimum of material security and freedom if it is to survive. In 445 a Jew named Nehemiah, who served the king of Persia in faraway Susa, heard about the misery of the city of his fathers: "The survivors there in the province who escaped exile are in great trouble and shame; the wall of Jerusalem is broken down, and its gates are destroyed by fire." (Neh. 1:3.) Nehemiah's conscience was deeply stirred: "I sat down and wept, and mourned for days; and I continued fasting and praying before the God of heaven." (Neh. 1:4.) God once more heard the cry of his People and sent them a deliverer. Nehemiah's reconstruction of the city walls is a grand story of faith. It shows how the conviction of one man can stir a whole people to action. His stand in the social conflict that threatens the community also shows that the burning sense of justice of the prophets is not dead (see Neh., ch. 5).

The eighth chapter of Nehemiah describes a great religious

assembly of Israel. The significant feature is that all, men and women, listen to the reading of "the book"—the Torah. A new era of preaching and teaching has begun. How wise are the readers! They know the book to be difficult: they "helped the people to understand the law. . . . They gave the sense, so that the people understood the reading" (Neh. 8:7-8).

This is where the real restoration takes place! God has spoken again with power and might to his People and this time through "the book." Because he is among them they are called first to be *joyful;* joyful in spite of the contrast between the dire reality and their hopes; joyful in spite of the fact that the law tells of great promises yet unfulfilled, of a covenant so many times broken: "'Do not be grieved, for the joy of the Lord is your strength.' . . . And all the people went their way to eat and drink and to send portions and to make great rejoicing, because they had understood the words that were declared to them." (Neh. 8:10, 12.)

They had understood. The restoration of Jerusalem was received as a sign of God's faithfulness, of his forgiveness. The Sabbath is a day of rejoicing. Later they meditated further on the law and confessed "their sins and the iniquities of their fathers" (Neh. 9:2). For God's People were one in space and time, bound by the same allegiance, and therefore sharing in both sin and forgiveness. The long story of God's call and forbearance and of Israel's betrayals was recapitulated and the covenant was "firmly" renewed (See Neh. 9:38). The new assembly of Israel was constituted as a gathered community of the faithful. Israel will know from now on, for nearly three centuries, what we, in our modern language, like to describe as "religious freedom." But with the Syrian king Antiochus Epiphanes, persecution begins and calls forth the Maccabean revolt. For a time Israel will again taste political independence (167 to 63 B.C.). This period begins well and ends in strife and dissension, calling for the intervention of the Roman Empire. In

Jesus' day there will still be a party—the Zealots—plotting for the recovery of independence. Jesus will be accused of being one of them even while he takes the firmest stand against them. He will prophesy the oncoming doom, as the ancient prophets had done, and the catastrophe will come in A.D. 70. Is all this a sign that Israel was intended to be not a nation "like all the nations" but God's People set apart to carry the message of salvation to the world?

The Worshiping Community

We have already seen that after the exile, the Temple took a central place in the worship of the returned Jews. Not only that, but the yearly festivals will for centuries to come, until A.D. 70, attract pilgrims from all the dispersed colonies of Jewry. We know that many of the psalms were hymns sung by the pilgrims going up to the Temple: the "Songs of Ascents" are the most well known of these (Ps. 120 to 134).

The Psalms—Israel's hymns—are one of the deepest expressions of the worship life of the community. While some are very ancient, and David is looked upon as the source of Israel's musical inspiration, the great development of hymnology seems to have taken place during the postexilic period. Many psalms have the character of an individual prayer, but the distress, the faith, the hope they express belong to the faithful people as a whole. They lay bare the soul of Israel, its waiting upon God, its anguish and its thankfulness. Praise and adoration of God are the dominant note of the Psalter. Creation glorifies him, history tells of his judgments and deliverances, and the individual soul rejoices in his salvation. Besides the love of the Temple and the God who dwelt there, the psalms stress the love of God's law. Psalms 19 and 119 do not see the law as a heavy burden laid on the conscience of the believer, but as a revelation of God's ways which revives the believer's soul and rejoices his heart:

"I will meditate on thy precepts,
    and fix my eyes on thy ways.
I will delight in thy statutes;
    I will not forget thy word. . . .
"The law of thy mouth is better to me
    than thousands of gold and silver pieces."
                        (Ps. 119:15-16, 72.)

Nowhere has the passionate love for God's will, the awareness of man's vocation as one of obedience to that will, been expressed in stronger terms or with such an inward longing as in this Ps. 119. The true Israelite loves God and his commandments with all his adoring heart and mind.

The psalmists had also, as we have seen all through, a deep sense of God's holiness, of his "otherness." This sense of distance will be stressed more and more in postexilic Judaism. It will go to the point of never pronouncing the name of the Most High — for the name evokes the Presence. And this Presence tends to be relegated to the Holy of Holies into which the high priest alone enters but once a year. This very holiness makes the priesthood an indispensable intermediary between God and his People. For the priest alone can present the offerings; he alone can perform the necessary rites of purification.

The attacks of the prophets upon an unfaithful priesthood which compromised with idolatry and indulged in the complacencies of a state religion, should not hide from us the great role of the priesthood in the preservation and interpretation of the tradition, in the maintenance and deepening of the faith. It is in priestly circles that some of the greatest theological insights of the Old Testament have been received and transmitted, and the word has come down to us as the Word of God through the instrumentality of both priest and prophet. The Pentateuch (Five Books of Moses) as well as the historical books combines the testimony of both traditions and this gives to the testimony its fullness and wholeness. (As an example, compare the first and second chapter of Genesis; each conveys specific aspects of the same truth.)

On the other hand, we must see the danger threatening all institutions, and specifically religious institutions — the danger of defeating their purpose by becoming ends in themselves. As they strive for self-perpetuation they too easily identify their existence with God's purpose. The party of the Sadducees which developed during the Maccabean period was deeply involved in political intrigues, and the survival of the Temple as an institution became, under Roman domination, the all-important factor. At the same time faith relaxed, and money-making became more important. Jesus, quoting a word of Jeremiah, accused the priesthood of his time of having changed his Father's house into " a den of robbers " (see Mark 11:17; Jer. 7:11). As over against the Sadducees, the Pharisees stressed strict obedience to God's law, and concentrated on the synagogue as a place both of worship and of teaching.

The Ingrown Community

We have seen that in the time of Israel's existence as a free nation, its constant temptation was toward assimilation, to be permeated, if not absorbed, by surrounding religions and cultures. When Israel reconstructs its spiritual home and national life after the exile, the same danger threatens, though in a less crude form. But this time there is among the returning flock a strong determination. The purity of the Yahwistic faith is to be preserved at all costs; all contacts with the surrounding peoples are to be avoided. This leads to the blunt refusal of any assistance for the reconstruction of the Temple and to an early conflict with the Samaritans. Not only must the priesthood be of pure blood, but the building of God's house is to be done exclusively by those who have kept the true faith. (See Ezra 2:59–63; 4:1–5. The Jews who had remained in the northern part of the country still claimed to believe in Yahweh but had developed a kind of syncretism.) One cannot but admire this intransigence when one knows how it exposed the whole enterprise to the risk of failure, and certainly delayed it for many years.

A more drastic measure is soon to be taken in the matter of mixed marriages. Such marriages had been one of the main causes of idolatry in the former kingdoms of Israel and Judah. Now, severe measures are decided upon. We are told that " the people wept bitterly. . . . And all the people sat in the open square before the house of God, trembling because of this matter and because of the heavy rain." (Ezra 10:1, 9; see also Neh. 13:23-31.) A pathetic picture of this dreary day when all stood shivering in both soul and body! But the thing is done. A census is taken. We are given the names of all the culprits. Ezra's memoirs close with the sober statement: " All these had married foreign women, and they put them away with their children." (Ezra 10:44.) Our modern mind wonders what became of all these wives and children, but there is no concern expressed by the Biblical writer! God is a stern surgeon who does not hesitate to cut the limb to save the body. Maybe our modern softness can learn something from this determination to put first things first, and first come God's will and God's Kingdom. The family unit can stand under God only if it is one in faith. (A problem as tragic as the one facing the Jews in Ezra's time is to be seen in the mission field when converts are not allowed to keep more than one wife. As Christians, we believe that in this case it is the church's duty to care for the rejected wives; it all too often happens that the only livelihood open to them is prostitution.)

Other measures are taken, concerning, for instance, the observance of the Sabbath. The zeal for keeping the Lord's commandments will soon lead to a puritanical legalism. Yet the deep meaning of the day of rest and rejoicing should not be forgotten.

In its anxiousness to preserve the integrity of the faith, post-exilic Judaism will develop into an ingrown, self-contented community. It will lose the great prophetic vision of its world-wide mission. Yet there will always be a few voices reminding it of its vocation. The story of Ruth, the Moabitess, is meant to show that a foreign woman can be a true Israelite. It is not by accident that she will be mentioned by name among Jesus' ancestors. The story of Jonah, running away from God because he does not want to be his messenger of doom to Nineveh, and even more displeased later when Nineveh is converted and forgiven, is a vivid satire on Judah's lack of interest in the fate of the nations — more, of its secret desire that the nations should not be converted! Such stories are the proof, once more, that God does not leave himself without witnesses. At the same time, they underline the general trend of the times toward narrow nationalism. Because the ambitions of the nation as such have been thwarted, the people find a new expression in the religious community as the preserver of tradition. In modern times, how often does the refugee or exile develop an exclusive attachment for his church as the one thing left that symbolizes for him his national tradition and culture!

Thus postexilic Judaism, with all the positive values we have already stressed, is threatened with becoming a faith imbued with nationalism on the one hand and legalism on the other. The extreme form of this legalism is to be found in the party of the Pharisees. Jesus' severe words are apt to make us consider all Pharisees as self-righteous hypocrites. This would be unfair. Jesus' attitude should be better compared to that of a modern preacher warning his congregation: "You who sit in the pews, you believe that you are better than others! But are you? You have received more and will be judged more severely!" The Pharisees had "separated" from the bulk of the people in order to submit themselves to a self-imposed discipline at a time of general religious and moral decadence. They were the exponents of the strict observance of the law. But their passion for the law led many of them to a kind of fanaticism. They developed a casuistry providing for an answer for every problem of behavior that might arise. They were filled with missionary zeal and traversed sea and land to make a single proselyte, but then they made him " a child of hell " (Matt. 23:15).

In other words, the Pharisees had all the exclusiveness, the forcefulness, and the spiritual pride which in all times characterize " the sect." They thought of themselves as the sole true worshipers of the Most High. They were the " saved " and all others were lost. They avoided all contacts with outcasts for fear of being defiled. Why did they make " children of hell " of their proselytes? Because their self-righteousness killed in them any understanding of God's grace and God's love. Theirs became a religion of works — demanding for themselves, merciless for others. And this desperate attempt to build up their own salvation and to behave as virtuous men tended finally to make them into " whitewashed tombs " (Matt. 23:27). Modern psychology strikingly confirms Jesus' observations on this point. Our suppressed feelings, our suppressed sense of guilt, destroy the soul more surely than any openly acknowledged sin.

Protestantism was born of Luther's reaction against a conception of salvation by works, and of his experience of justification by faith alone as the gospel's great message of reconciliation and deliverance. But there is a striking tendency in the history of Protestantism, especially Calvinist Protestantism, to revert in practice to the legalistic tendency of Judaism. It is the mark of legalism to lay stress on the law as a code of behavior, until law finally becomes a means of salvation, a substitute for the gospel. Where this happens, a new kind of pharisaism develops and the joy of salvation is lost. This joy of God which the Old Testament, at its best, already knew, will ring all through the apostolic proclamation. It is not among the Pharisees, but among the poor and humble of heart that " God made man " will choose his dwelling place. These are the true remnant, the Israel after God's heart, waiting for his Day.

CHAPTER IX

In the Fullness of Time — The Messianic Community

*" Blessed be the God and Father of our Lord Jesus Christ.
. . . For he has made known to us in all wisdom and insight the mystery of his will, according to his purpose which
he set forth in Christ as a plan for the fullness of time, to
unite all things in him, things in heaven and things on
earth."* (Eph. 1:3, 9–10.)

We have seen in our studies of the Old Testament how God
worked through *a People*. We have seen how this People was
called by its very existence to bear witness to God's sovereignty
and justice, and above all to God's redeeming purpose among
the nations. Of course, God sets apart certain men for a specific
service: Abraham, Moses, David, the prophets. But these men
are never isolated individuals. Abraham starts his venture of
faith with his family; he is called as the father of the tribe which
is to be born of him. Moses is called as the mediator who will
deliver God's People from bondage and lead them to the Promised Land. David is called as God's anointed to watch over the
newborn nation. The priest brings the offerings to the altar as
the representative of the people. The prophet is God's voice sum-
moning His People to repentance and newness of life. This
does not mean that there is not in every case a very personal
relationship with God; but it does mean that the individual acts
as a member of the community.

In the postexilic period individual salvation is more frequently stressed. But it has often been noticed that when the psalmist praises God and sings of his deliverance, he does so as a member of the community and constantly passes from the singular to the plural because he identifies his own cause with that of God's People.

When Jesus enters the scene of history he proclaims the *Kingdom of God,* God's Kingship, *God's rule,* and places the accent on *God.* Salvation means turning from self-centeredness to God-centeredness; it means concretely becoming a member of the Messianic community which has the signs and tokens of the oncoming Kingdom. The law is summarized by Jesus as well as by the rabbis of his time in love of God and love of neighbor, these being aspects of one and the same reality. More than that: the Son of Man embodies Israel, he is the true Israel — the king, priest, and prophet of the new dispensation. And he will call a " new Israel " into being. This is shown in the fact that the whole terminology of the New Testament is reminiscent of the exodus. A new People is going to be born, a People declared to be the royal priests and prophets of the new dispensation. To be a Christian is *ipso facto* to be a member of this newborn community. The choice of twelve apostles is a reminder of the twelve tribes and shows clearly that Jesus intends to build the true Israel. We shall try now to examine briefly the way in which Jesus himself conceived this new community.

The New Community

John the Baptist's message is a call to repentance because the Kingdom is *at hand.* John's stern call is akin to Amos' message in the eighth century. The Lord's Day will be a day of judgment. Israel is to believe and repent, or perish. Jesus starts his preaching with a similar message. " The time is fulfilled, and the kingdom of God is at hand; repent, and believe in the gospel." (Mark 1:15.) But now the stress is on *fulfillment.*

There is in Israel a " remnant " which awaits the Messianic

times. The figures of Simeon and Anna in Luke are symbolic of those "poor in Israel" who awaited the promised deliverance. It is among the "poor," the humble of heart, that this expectation runs highest. It is among these "humble of heart" that Jesus finds his first followers — fishermen, taxgatherers, men and women of little standing in the religious community of their time. Again, as in olden times, God calls those of no status to form the nucleus of his People. Thirty years later Paul writes to the Corinthians: "Consider your call, brethren; not many of you were wise according to worldly standards, not many were powerful, not many were of noble birth; but God chose what is foolish in the world to shame the wise, God chose what is weak in the world to shame the strong, God chose what is low and despised in the world, even things that are not, to bring to nothing things that are, so that no human being might boast in the presence of God." (I Cor. 1:26-29.) When God wants to make a new start and build his People, his policy stands in strange contrast with our worldly ways: "He has put down the mighty from their thrones, and exalted those of low degree." (Luke 1:52.)

As he took Moses out of the bulrushes to overcome Pharaoh, as he called slave tribes to become his People, so does God choose a humble woman of Nazareth to be the mother of his Son, a stable to be his birthplace. There is a deep symbolism in Herod's attempt to kill the child Jesus and in the story of the holy family's flight to Egypt. God's hand is once again on those "of low degree" as over against the rulers of this world. The Son of Man will have no place to rest his head. The religious leaders of Israel will look down upon the Nazarene. "What good can come from Nazareth?"

The King who comes unto his own comes, from the very beginning, in the figure of a servant, totally ignored by the great of this world (the Herods excepted!). Never was an incognito better kept. He whom Christians regard as the clue to all history lived and died without any Roman historian's taking notice of his existence. To Rome, his death remained among the *faits divers* of current policy in an occupied country.

This is God's way of working: a great lesson to us who yearn for spectacular results! Jesus gathers a few followers, people he has cured from diseases, women whose lost dignity he has restored. And many come who will leave him at the end.

The King's Charter

The Sermon on the Mount (Matt., chs. 5 to 7), which exalts the poor and the meek, is the *charter of the new community he calls into being.* "It was said . . . but I say to you." The so-called Sermon on the Mount echoes Deutero-Isaiah in many ways. The promise of God is to the poor, the meek, those who hunger and thirst for righteousness, the merciful, the sons of peace. To them belongs the Kingdom. They shall inherit the earth. The Sermon on the Mount raises many problems. Is it *a law?* It has sometimes been so interpreted, by Tolstoy, for instance. At the other extreme are those who stress the *impossibility* of the claim: they compare these commandments to a wall that we cannot climb. We can only interpret the Sermon on the Mount in the light of Him *who lived it.* He alone can work in us the change of heart implied in every one of his commandments.

It is our very *motives* that must be changed. "Be perfect, as your heavenly Father is perfect." (Matt. 5:48.) It is in the power of the Christ who lived the Sermon and conquered sin and death to build us into his likeness. The claims of the Sermon on the Mount are a constant challenge to our ways of living and thinking. They throw us back on God's mercy. But this is not enough. Jesus really intends the little company of his followers, the Messianic community, to follow his way. "No one can serve two masters." (Matt. 6:24.) Those who follow him must leave behind their nets, their houses, their fathers and mothers. " Seek first his kingdom and his righteousness." (Matt. 6:33.) There is a radical choice to be made.

Does not the weakness of our churches lie in the fact that we have dulled the edge of the radical challenge of the Gospels? Is there that extraordinary quality in our communities which makes them utterly different from secular groups? The new community is to bear some of the signs of the Kingdom to come.

The Kingdom — Present or Future?

Jesus' interpretation of the Kingdom of God is a controversial matter. Personally, we have no doubt that for him it was both *a present and a future reality*. Where the King is, there God's Kingship unfolds its power. Where diseases are healed, where demons are cast out, where sinners repent, the Kingdom is manifested.

The Messianic community has the tokens of the Kingdom to come. The disciples are to go and heal the sick and say, "The kingdom of God has come near to you" (Luke 10:9). Christ's very appearance in this world means *decision* — radical decision for or against him, for or against the Kingdom he proclaims. The Messianic community is the nucleus committed to his new way of life. It is the "little flock" to which it pleases the Father to give the Kingdom. The group of disciples is still very fragile in its faith, very limited in its understanding. But it has left all things behind to follow Christ. This is the all-important fact.

The Way of the Servant

To those who ask for "signs," Jesus answers that "the kingdom of God is not coming with signs to be observed" (Luke 17:20). Of all Messianic expectations he has chosen the least understood, the least popular, the way of the *Suffering Servant*. In so doing, he destroys all the nationalistic hopes of the Zealot, all the apocalyptic hopes of the Pharisee (at least for the immediate future). The acceptance of the way of the cross as a necessary one means a long struggle, and anguish of soul. The Synoptics have preserved for us the memory of this anguish in the story of the temptation and in Jesus' rebuke to Peter, " Get behind me, Satan! " (Matt. 16:23); in his solitary walk toward Jerusalem when he knows that his " exodus " is to take place; in the Garden of Olives; in his cry, " My God, my God, why hast thou forsaken me? " (Matt. 27:46). If proof were needed of the truthfulness of the Gospel records, it should be found in these texts where Jesus appears in his full humanity, so very far from any stoic resignation. He has really " taken our flesh." He has struggled to know and accept the will of God. He has gone down to the last depths of desolation.

Jesus has come to the conviction that his death was not only inescapable but necessary in God's plan for the salvation of mankind. " For the Son of man also came not to be served but to serve, and to give his life as a ransom for many." (Mark 10:45.) The Last Supper marks clearly the connection between his death and the salvation of his People: " My body which is for you." (I Cor. 11:24.) Jesus never explained this mystery of the substitution of " One for many." This thought of vicarious action was so rooted in the Jewish tradition that it did not need much explanation. Had not " all " been baptized into Moses in the Red Sea? Was not every Jew to look upon himself as sharing in the once-achieved deliverance, as *included* in the Sinai covenant?

The Suffering Servant of Isaiah is certainly present to Jesus' mind. The time will come when his disciples will understand the meaning of this *new covenant* sealed with his blood. But there is one thing Jesus makes clear to his disciples from the very first: his way, the way of suffering, the way of the cross, is also to be *their way*. It was already implied in the Beatitudes. It is strongly stressed in the three Synoptic Gospels after his announcement of his coming death. The saying about losing one's life in order to find it is quoted five times in the four Gospels.

Jesus and Israel

What attitude did Jesus take toward Israel as the *chosen People* of God?

We cannot discard certain sayings of Matthew which stress the primary concern of Jesus for his own People as the chosen People of God. Their responsibility is *unique*, because of their election. They are not so much his nation as his church. Jesus has taken a stand against the nationalist movement of his time. He has acknowledged the occupying power as having certain rights: give to Caesar what is Caesar's (see Matt. 22:21). He says to Pilate that his power is given him from above. He even says to his disciples, "If any one forces you to go one mile, go with him two miles" (Matt. 5:41), and this means to carry the burden of a soldier, of a Roman legionary. A hard saying in an occupied land!

No, his love for Israel has nothing to do with nationalism; it is the "last call" to a rebellious People. This is best illustrated by the parable of the husbandman (Mark 12:1–10), Jesus' last sad call to Jerusalem (see Matt. 23:37–39; Luke 19:41–44). There is strong evidence that his first preaching was concentrated on "the lost sheep of . . . Israel" (Matt. 15:24). But just because of the depth of his concern for Israel, Jesus' scorn turns against the scribes and Pharisees as the spiritual leaders in Israel. They have laid heavy burdens on others and do not carry the burdens themselves. They have killed the spirit and kept the letter. Judaism has become a self-satisfied *ghetto religion.* Jesus fights against Pharisaic legalism with the vigor of the old prophets of Israel. No word is too harsh to condemn that kind of religion. They are "whitewashed tombs" (Matt. 23:27), decorated without, dead within.

The conflict started early. According to the Gospel of Mark, it began at the very first of his ministry. The freedom of Jesus in his relations with all men, including the outcasts, the publicans, and prostitutes, his healing on the Sabbath, his utterances, his whole attitude, are a scandal to the rigid Pharisees. Certainly traditionalism and spiritual pride have something to do with this. But the conflict goes deeper. The Pharisee's theology — more, his whole way of salvation — is called in question. There are two groups of men for whom Jesus can do nothing: the materially secure who cling to their goods, and the spiritually secure who cling to their systems and institutions. As Jeremiah prophesied the destruction of a desecrated Temple in 600 B.C., so does Jesus foresee the destruction of the new Temple, the grand building erected by Herod the Great. He knows that soon there will not remain " stone upon stone " (Matt. 24:2). The new worship is to be a worship in spirit and in truth.

Though Jesus is rejected by the spiritual leaders of his People, his ministry points to another fact: his gospel means salvation to the lost, to the despised. Not only the Jewish outcasts, but also the pagans respond to his message. The Roman centurion amazes Jesus by his simple, straightforward faith: " Truly, I say to you, not even in Israel have I found such faith. I tell you, many will come from east and west and sit at table with Abraham, Isaac, and Jacob in the kingdom of heaven, while the sons of the kingdom will be thrown into the outer darkness; there men will weep and gnash their teeth." (Matt. 8:10–12.) Here again Jesus stands in line with the great prophetic expectation. The succession in Israel is not of the flesh but of the faith. There are no borders confining the Kingdom except those of faith in and allegiance to the King.

King and Judge

The passage that gives us deepest insight into the breadth and nature of the oncoming Kingdom is probably the parable of the Last Judgment (Matt. 25:31–46). Here we see the Son of Man coming in glory, in Kingly might and grandeur. Before him stand the nations. And the King who is judge says to those on his right hand:

"'Come, O blessed of my Father, inherit the kingdom prepared for you from the foundation of the world; for I was hungry and you gave me food, I was thirsty and you gave me drink, I was a stranger and you welcomed me, I was naked and you clothed me, I was sick and you visited me, I was in prison and you came to me.' Then the righteous will answer him, 'Lord, when did we see thee hungry and feed thee, or thirsty and give thee drink? And when did we see thee a stranger and welcome thee, or naked and clothe thee? And when did we see thee sick or in prison and visit thee?' And the King will answer them, 'Truly, I say to you, as you did it to one of the least of these my brethren, you did it to me.'" (Matt. 25:34–40.)

Who are these blessed ones? The "nations" in Biblical thought are the pagans. Who are the "little ones"? Only believers? No, all the downtrodden of the earth. What is done to them is done to the Son of Man. Why? Not "as if," but *because* the Son of Man is the representative of mankind. He has taken concretely upon himself the suffering and sin of *every human being*. He has identified himself with every one of them. The crucified and risen Lord can say in regard to every man, "What you have done to him you have done to me." A terrible affirmation! What we, Christians, all through history have done or allowed to be done to the Jews, to the slaves, to the subject peoples, to the deported in concentration camps, to the refugees, we have done to *Him*. All we have not done to them we have not done to him. And he will face us in the last day with that "you did it to me." Here is the real basis of Christian ethics: every human being is a man for whom Christ died, a man whose suffering and death Jesus has taken upon himself. Atonement does not mean anything if it does not mean Christ's at-one-ness with all humanity's misery and sinfulness.

I do not think we can limit this at-one-ness to those who are consciously members of his body. He died in order "to draw all men to himself," taking them with him in his death and his resurrection. He can do this because he is the true *Israel,* Son of God and Son of Man, standing vicariously for all.

"Here Is the Man"

Pilate says of him: "Here is the man!" (John 19:5.) The trial of Jesus shows us the reality of man. Here stands Man as God wills him, truly made "in the image of God," showing forth as in a perfect mirror God's righteousness and love. And here also stands mankind. The only *free* one is the one who is bound. All others are captives, bound by spiritual pride and a hard and fast theology which refuses to be challenged (as to this man, "we do not know where he comes from"! [John 9:29]). Bound by the secular interests of the religious institutions ("It is expedient for you that one man should die for the people"! [John 11:50]). Bound by personal and state interests ("If you release this man, you are not Caesar's friend"! [John 19:12]). Bound by the fear of being denounced ("You also were with the Nazarene" [Mark 14:67]). Bound by an anonymous mob reaction ("The chief priests stirred up the crowd" and "they shouted" [Mark 15:11, 14]). How in this brief scene all the weakness and cowardice of mankind are laid bare! How triumphantly the "ruler of this world" rules over them all! Jesus stands alone. And in one word he reveals the secret of his freedom: "The ruler of this world . . . has no power over me." (John 14:30.)

Once in history a Man lived whose freedom was perfect freedom, whose love was perfect love. And mankind could not endure him; his very presence became unbearable. This is why the cross stands in judgment not over the Jews alone, nor merely over the Roman Empire and its magistrates, but over our whole humanity. Here, only here, are our thoughts stripped naked. Here, only here, do all masks fall. Here, only here, is our chance to see ourselves as we are and to accept the verdict. Here, only here, can the real meaning of God's mercy be discovered. Here One dies for all that all may believe and live.

Here the Word is made flesh and God "tabernacles" among men. It belongs to the Gospel of John to put into words the mystery of the Son of Man, where the Synoptics simply give the facts. The Fourth Gospel sees each concrete deed as a sign and symbol of an ultimate reality. All the great promises of the Old Testament are now fulfilled. Here is the new Temple of God where his glory shines. Here is the Paschal Lamb offered for the sins of the world. Here is the new manna, the Bread of Life. Here is the source of living water which quenches forever the thirst of the pilgrim People of God. Here is the Shepherd who gathers all the scattered sheep in his Father's house. Here is the true Vine, the life of which flows in the body of believers.

It is a striking thing that the images, symbols, events of the exodus and the prophets should thus be taken up and transferred to the person of Christ. Nearly all of them are to be found in the Synoptics, but the Fourth Gospel is more explicit and brings out their whole theological significance. The *vocation of the People of God is both embodied and fulfilled in Christ.* He is the *true Israel,* or, to speak with the book of Revelation, "*the* faithful witness" (Rev. 1:5). "He who has seen me has seen the Father." (John 14:9.) God in Christ has kept the covenant and paid the price for sin.

As the vocation of God's People is now transferred to Christ, so does Christ transfer the responsibility of witnessing to his disciples. As he is the light of the world, so are they now to be the light of the world and the salt of the earth. The members of the Messianic community are to be his witnesses to the ends of the world; yet it is not they who witness but the Holy Spirit in and through them. There is a transfer of authority and power which puzzles and frightens us. We know all too well what the disciples were: people, sore afraid, constantly misunderstanding their Master. And yet Jesus declares, "He who receives you receives me, and he who receives me receives him who sent me" (Matt. 10:40).

"Truly, truly, I say to you, he who believes in me will also do the works that I do; and greater works than these will he do, because I go to the Father. Whatever you ask in my name, I will do it, that the Father may be glorified in the Son; if you ask anything in my name, I will do it." (John 14:12–14.)

These words of the Gospel of John stress the fact that Jesus' return to the Father does not mean an end but an enlargement of his activity. He is no longer bound in the categories of space and time. What his church asks for, he will do, and there are no limits to his power, save those set by our lack of faith.

Indeed the story of the apostolic church is a " demonstration of the Spirit and power " (I Cor. 2:4).

CHAPTER X

The Great Proclamation: Christ Is Lord

"They were all filled with the Holy Spirit and spoke the word of God with boldness." (Acts 4:31.)

The Passion story leaves us with the picture of a few disheartened disciples whose hopes have been shattered. They go back to their fields or their fishing nets. The Master is dead, the Kingdom has not come, and this is the end.

The book of The Acts tells about a church filled with the Spirit, proclaiming the good news of salvation to the whole world. Jesus, crucified under Pontius Pilate, has revealed himself to his disciples as the living Lord. He has conquered sin and death!

How did this great certainty come to the disciples? The stories of Christ's appearance raise problems for the New Testament scholar. There remains a veil of mystery on the " how " of the Lord's resurrection. He enters the upper room through closed doors. He eats broiled fish with his disciples and has them touch his body. The details vary and no attempt has been made in the Gospel records to unify the story. How thankful we should be to the church for that! For a living faith, material details are secondary. If a proof of the resurrection were needed, it would be found in the very existence of the church. For without the two events of the resurrection and the outpouring of the Spirit, both its witness and its life would be inexplicable.

Opening Their Minds

The New Testament is sober in its account of the period between the Lord's resurrection and Pentecost. Yet at the end of this period the disciples have reached three great certainties: (1) Jesus is risen from the dead and sits "at the right hand of God," which means that he occupies the place that earthly monarchs reserve to the heir who shares in their power and glory; (2) the death of Jesus has vicarious meaning; (3) all that has happened is witnessed by the Scriptures to be the fulfillment of God's eternal promises.

The brief accounts of Luke and Acts show that the time between Easter and Pentecost was a time of inner preparation in which the disciples, having received the revelation that their Lord lives, pray and search the Scriptures in order to grasp the meaning of the events through which they have passed. The risen Lord gives them the great commission: to be his witnesses to the end of the earth. From now on this is their *raison d'être*, their life motivation. And "witness" has here the double meaning of an eyewitness and of one who is able to interpret what he has seen. The apostles have been eyewitnesses of Jesus' earthly life and trial. But by revealing himself to them as the risen Lord, Jesus has also introduced them into the heavenly court where God has "justified" his Servant by raising him from the dead and glorifying him (Acts 1:8; see also Acts 3:13-15). Jesus is the Fulfiller in whom all the prophets of the Old Testament find their accomplishment. But he is also the One in whom all Scriptures have their ultimate meaning, so that he will become for the church the sole valid interpreter of Scriptures, in whom and through whom "the veil" is lifted (II Cor. 3:14-16). This "Christocentric" interpretation of Scripture is common to all New Testament writers. It will guide the exegesis of the fathers of the church. We are aware that the principle has sometimes been carried too far: sayings of the Old Testament have been forced into a strait jacket, or allegorized, in order to make them fit into a Christological interpretation. On the other hand, the historical school of the nineteenth century missed the real meaning of the Biblical message when it reduced Biblical accounts to the dimensions of historical events, without seeing their interrelatedness and the God-given direction in which they point. The Old Testament is an open, unfinished story. For a Christian its real meaning can only be seen in the light of its fulfillment in Christ. And Christ helps us to see both what should be dropped and what should be retained of Old Testament claims. The problem is really whether we read the Old Testament as Christians for whom the incarnation is the center of, and the key to, all history.

We have evidence of this reinterpretation of the Scriptures in Peter's discourse related in the second chapter of Acts. It is entirely built on Scripture references. While this speech should not be taken as a shorthand copy of the words pronounced, it certainly reproduces the essential lines of apostolic preaching. And it concludes with the confession, " Let all the house of Israel therefore know assuredly that God has made him both Lord and Christ, this Jesus whom you crucified " (Acts 2:36).

We can only understand how startling such a statement sounded when we remember that Jesus had been killed a few weeks before; that his was a most ignominious death (" Cursed be every one who hangs on a tree," Gal. 3:13), and that his mission seemed to have ended in utter failure. We have here probably the most ancient confession of the church's faith: *this* Jesus is *Lord!* Paul writes to the Corinthians, " For I delivered to you as of first importance what I also received, that Christ died for our sins in accordance with the scriptures, that he was buried, that he was raised on the third day in accordance with the scriptures, and that he appeared to Cephas, then to the twelve " (I Cor. 15:3-5). The resurrection is the glorious proof that Christ's death was not that of a criminal nor that of a martyr, but that of the Servant fulfilling his God-given mission, the

Suffering Servant of Isaiah offering his life as a ransom for many. This is the common profession of faith of the whole apostolic church.

The Baptism of the Spirit

Jesus had made the reception of the Holy Spirit a precondition of his disciples' witness " to the end of the earth " (Acts 1:8). It is the descending of the Holy Spirit on the apostles on Pentecost Day that creates the church. We do not mean, of course, that the church did not exist before that. Jesus had started gathering the " little flock " during his earthly ministry; he had called the Twelve and given them their missionary commission. But it is on Pentecost Day that the divine seal is laid on the new People of God — God's holy Tribe! — as the fellowship of the Spirit, as the new community which is now to be both the instrument and the token of God's saving purpose.

Already, through the coming into existence of this community, the new era has begun. The Spirit is seen as a power from God entering this world and announcing thereby the renewal of all things. The apostle Peter sees in this breaking in of the Spirit a fulfillment of Joel's prophecy. The " last days " have come, when God's Spirit will be poured upon all flesh (see Acts 2:16–21). In other words, the church, while pursuing its earthly career, has already, through the Spirit, the tokens of the Kingdom.

It seems certain that the early Christians expected Christ to return soon, and that they believed the end of the present world to be near. But the time factor is secondary: " With the Lord one day is as a thousand years, and a thousand years as one day." (II Peter 3:8.) What matters is that the decisive event, Christ's coming in the flesh, has taken place. The church is aware of standing now in an utterly new situation, between the fulfillment of God's purpose in history and the manifestation of that fulfillment. He who has come in the incognito of the Servant will come as the King of Glory. For the church which be-lieves in him he is already the King of Glory and his Spirit is at work. Thus the church stands "between the times." It is the expectant church which awaits the new realm but at the same time proclaims a victory already achieved, a salvation already assured. This joyful assurance rings through its message on Pentecost Day and ever after.

The meaning of this "interim period" is clear: it is the time assigned to the church for proclaiming the good news to the whole world. This is its central task on earth (see Acts 1:8; Matt. 24:14; 28:19-20). In this regard the vocation of the "New Israel" differs from that of the Old. Old Israel was the city on the hill to which, one day, the nations would flock. It did not go out of its way to make converts. Judaism in Jesus' time certainly had proselytes, but they remained second-class be-lievers unless they submitted to circumcision and all the pre-scriptions of the law.

Now, *the time of gathering and harvesting* announced by Jesus has begun. Pentecost is symbolic of this gathering; the Holy Spirit unites the scattered Jews of the Dispersion and makes them one. The story is the counterpart of the Tower of Babel. Unity built from beneath ended in dispersion and chaos. True unity has to come from above. This is very important for all our thinking about church unity. To build unity on the hu-man level by diplomatic conversations and compromise will al-ways mean a shaky construction. The broken church can be restored only from above. This does not exclude our constant striving for mutual understanding, our common searching for truth. But to restore unity, more than this is needed. The work of Christ's Spirit, humbling and sifting, pruning and purifying, breaking through our stubborn oppositions and making all things new, is necessary. When one asks whether we believe that the divided churches will ever unite on earth, and *how* they can unite, we can only answer: "I believe in the Holy Spirit" and " I believe in one holy catholic church." When and how the unity of this one church will be manifested on the historical level of existing churches is the secret of God, and the way in which it will happen is to be left to him. Our task is to pray and to strive and to enter into an ever-deepening relation with the living Christ, the Lord of the one church.

The Spirit manifests his power through certain outward signs such as speaking in tongues. Yet much more significant is his *witnessing function.* The people assembled in Jerusalem during the feast hear in their own tongue about " the mighty works of God " (Acts 2:6, 11). The preaching of Peter is presented as an act of power which *cuts people to the heart,* so that they ask, " Brethren, what shall we do? " (Acts 2:37.) (None of them could have gone out saying, " What a nice sermon we have heard today! ") Where the Spirit is at work, decisions have to be made.

All through Acts the Spirit is the real actor and men are his instruments: in the strength of his power they preach, they heal, they face their opponents. There lies a deep significance in the fact that the outpouring of the Holy Spirit immediately means two things: the power of " communication " which forces the world to listen to the gospel, and the coming into existence of a community.

The thought that under the new dispensation God's temple is no more a building of stone but the worshiping and witnessing community of believers, and that it is called to be a temple of the Spirit, is developed later in the letters of Paul and Peter. But the fact is already given in the early chapters of Acts. While the disciples are still faithful Jews assembling in the Temple for prayer, a community develops, having a life of its own, a " fellowship of the Spirit."

The vocation and activity of the new community described in Acts (chs. 2; 4:32-37) can be summarized in three words: proclamation, fellowship, service. None of these English words renders fully the meaning of the Greek words: *ķērygma, ķoinōnia, diaķonia*. By *ķērygma* we should understand the preached, proclaimed message of the church. *Koinōnia* is a " togetherness," a sharing in the common life, but a common life based on a common loyalty. *Diaķonia* is the service of the brethren understood as a mutual obligation.

We should never forget that it is the *preaching* of the gospel which lays the foundations of the community. This is shown not only in the early chapters of Acts but all through the apostles' missionary work: "How are they to believe in him of whom they have never heard? And how are they to hear without a preacher?" (Rom. 10:14.) (Let us remember that one can sit in the pew for years and yet never have "heard.") God has done something about his world. The church's primary function is to proclaim his deeds to every generation, to confess its faith in him, and to laud and glorify him for what he has done. The New Testament testifies that the apostles' preaching rang with this note of certainty and joy. Their Christ is *Christus Victor*.

The churches of the Reformation claim to be the churches of the Word. Are they? Is it God's Word that comes down from the pulpit, "cutting the heart" of those who listen, or is it human words dictated by human wisdom? (We should like to refer the reader on this point to Prof. Donald G. Miller's book *Fire in Thy Mouth*, Abingdon Press, 1954.) The preacher's task is a hard one, because he must hold the two-edged sword which cuts the hand of him who handles it. Always he must first receive what he is going to give out. It is the function of a praying church to bear up the servant in charge of the proclamation, and to hear what God wills to say through him as a word from God and not from man. In a living church there is a secret and deep relation, a constant give-and-take, between the preacher and the community.

We are told that those who were gathered by Peter's preach-

ing and had received baptism " devoted themselves to the apostles' teaching " (Acts 2:42). Teaching is the second step. Here
again one might say that a lot of " education " goes on in the
churches. Is it always " apostolic "? When one has the opportunity to talk with laymen of all walks of life, one cannot help
being appalled at their ignorance of the Scriptures. The Scriptures were the basis of apostolic teaching. And how often such
laymen confess and deplore their ignorance! The Bible is a
difficult book; instruction is needed. In the twenties, at a time
when the Bible was neglected and considered, even in Christian
circles, as somewhat out of date, a student cried out, " Give us
steak!" There are many thoughtful laymen today who want
solid meat instead of too many hors d'oeuvres.

> " ' Behold, the days are coming,' says the Lord God,
>   ' when I will send a famine on the land;
>   not a famine of bread, nor a thirst for water,
>   but of hearing the words of the Lord.' "
>   (Amos 8:11.)

It is our firm conviction that such hunger exists in many parts
of the earth. Will the end of the prophet's sentence come true?

> " They shall wander from sea to sea,
>   and from north to east;
>   they shall run to and fro, to seek the word of the Lord,
>   but they shall not find it."
>   (Amos 8:12.)

" And they devoted themselves to [or " persevered in "] the
apostles' teaching and *fellowship,* to the breaking of bread and
the prayers." (Acts 2:42.) It is not quite clear whether the breaking of the bread " in their homes " (Acts 2:46) means the love
feast, the fraternal meal that we see practiced later in Corinth,
or whether the memorial of the Lord's Supper was at the beginning celebrated in the homes, where the Christians gathered for
prayer. It should be remembered that they had no place of wor-

ship of their own. And had not the Passover meal been a family celebration? We are told that the newborn community shared all things, material and spiritual. The "communism" of the Jerusalem church has been much discussed. That the new faith should open the hearts, and therefore the purse, seems normal (or should be). That not all gave up all their property and belongings, and that it was no imposed rule to do so, is shown by the examples given in Acts 4:36 to 5:11. But that no one was left needy is a sign of the spontaneous generosity of the community. Let us note that on this point they followed the best Old Testament tradition. Should the new Tribe prove less brotherly than the old? It seems to have been normal in these early days to welcome the brother in the faith at the family table. And how could one "break the bread" with him without commemorating the Lord's solemn words? Had he not promised that where two or three were assembled in his name, he would be present among them? Had not the disciples of Emmaus recognized him in the breaking of the bread? Had he not told them to break the bread in memory of his death, of his body offered for them, until he comes again?

May we not believe that in this simple act of the "breaking of the bread," the early Christians were aware of partaking not only in the Last Supper but also in the resurrection meal? More, of announcing the banquet of the Kingdom? The three events were thus actualized in the gathering of the fellowship. The holy Presence stood at the very center of their worship, and of their daily life.

We are aware of treading here on delicate ground. The example of Corinth shows that a time would inevitably come when the church would have to interfere in order to preserve the sacrament from profanation. But how tragically have we drifted away from the primitive simplicity of Christ's love feast! The sign of unity, the token of our oneness as partakers of his body and blood, has become the sign of our divisions, the greatest stumbling block on the path to unity. Never has the devil won a greater victory!

We should not idealize the primitive church. Very early we see divisions and strife appearing in its midst. This is human sin. But, this being said, we should also be sensitive to the freshness of these early stories. The birth of the church was a blessed act of God. The young church bursts with thankfulness, vigor, and joy. Such outbursts recur in church history. Where the Spirit moves, there is life and expansion, there is true love.

We should also see that in these early days of the church, as in the days of the old covenant, there is no line drawn between " sacred " and " profane," between cleric and layman. There is only one baptism and all are equally, in the sight of God, forgiven sinners, saved by grace. There are, of course, different functions, and apostolic authority is unquestioned. But God's claim is as total on every member of the church as it was on every member of the covenanted People.

And while the apostles carried a specific responsibility in the proclamation of the gospel, it is remarkable to what extent its spread in the whole Mediterranean world was due to the testimony of simple Christians — merchants, artisans, soldiers, and slaves, carrying the good news all through the Empire. In fact, the apostles' function was often to consolidate the work already begun (as, for instance, in Samaria). A living church is missionary in its very essence: its members cannot keep to themselves a faith that has changed their lives. The early church stands as a tiny minority in a hostile world. Theirs is the realistic fellowship of the battlefront. All share in the same faith, the same hope, the same dangers.

Sent to the End of the World

We have already mentioned the fact that the church in Jerusalem still stood within Judaism. Its members were faithful to the law and to the Temple worship. They must have appeared

THE GREAT PROCLAMATION: CHRIST IS LORD

rather as a " sect " than as the adherents of a new faith. How
slow we are at all times to see God's world-wide purposes! The
words of Jesus had not opened the eyes of the leaders in Jerusalem to the scope of their mission. The conversion of Cornelius
came to them as a shock (Acts, chs. 10; 11)! And with what
reluctance they were to accept Paul's call as apostle to the Gentiles, with all the consequences it implied! Provincialism is not
one of the least sins of the church — in all times. Sacred traditions were to be left behind. Opening the door to the outside
world would increase difficulties at home, and the whole of
Jewry would resist the new faith with increased violence. In
fact, it did. But God forced the doors to open when many would
have liked to keep them closed. The dispersion of the disciples
throughout Judea and Samaria, and as far as Cyprus and Antioch of Syria, started a movement that no earthly power could
stop.

And then God struck his decisive blow! He took Saul the
Pharisee, the zealous defender of the law, and made of him
Saint Paul. The story of Paul's world mission is an extraordi-
narily enlightening and stimulating one. His letters must be
read against the background of the missionary career that took
him from Antioch of Syria to the heart of Asia Minor, to
Greece, to Rome, and possibly to Spain. For nothing is more
unfair than to see Paul first and foremost as theologian. He is
the greatest theologian who ever lived; but he is first and foremost a missionary and a church builder. The very vigor of his
theological utterances lies in the fact that they are the fruit of
his personal encounter with God and of his missionary experience. He is a man of the frontier, Christ's herald in an alien
world.

There is scarcely a problem in the missionary work of the
church today of which we do not find a foretaste in Paul's
epistles. His methods would be worth a long study: the way in
which he builds up a nucleus by preaching and teaching; his

care to maintain his financial independence — even to earn his own living. On one point he is amazingly daring: the quickness with which he forces his young churches to stand on their own feet. He stays with them for a few weeks, or at most a few months; persecution or further calls draw him away. His longest stays are a year and a half in Corinth, two years in Ephesus. He must move on, in order to proclaim the gospel where it has not yet been announced! He sends emissaries, he writes letters, sometimes he burns with fever when he thinks of his churches. But he trusts God who has called these feeble Christians to complete what he has begun. A great lesson for us today!

We are privileged to live in a century when the church is recovering its sense of mission as a whole church to the whole world. We must be humble enough to recognize that this awareness of " the world " seen as a whole has imposed itself in this century on politicians, economists, and businessmen and is no special insight of ours. Distances have shrunk and the globe has shrunk in proportion. But the call is all the more urgent to go everywhere where the gospel has not yet been proclaimed, be it in the center of Africa or in the Western workshop. For our time for doing so may be short!

In many countries today the Christians are still — or are again —a tiny minority. We are in a situation more and more like that of the early church in the pagan world (we are aware that this is at present less true of North America than of most countries of Europe). We must learn from it what it means to proclaim God's Word. The pagan world of the first century can scarcely have been more skeptical or more disillusioned than ours. We must learn what it means to be a living fellowship of both worship and service. Our world hungers for fellowship! We must learn what it means to be " a witness " in whatever walk of life God has placed us.

CHAPTER XI

The Apostolic View of History

"'I am the Alpha and the Omega,' says the Lord God, who is and who was and who is to come, the Almighty."
(Rev. 1:8.)

We have seen that one essential aspect of the ancient prophets' message was their view of history. This message could be summarized as follows: (1) God is Lord of history; therefore history has meaning, it leads somewhere. (2) The Day of God's coming will be a Day of Judgment as well as renewal. (3) There will be an ultimate deliverance, a new creation; God's justice and mercy will prevail. (4) The new realm will be brought about by the Anointed, the Messiah. Power and judgment will belong to the sons of the Most High.

It is the task of the apostolic church to rethink and restate the vision of history in the light of its fulfillment in Christ. The redeeming act of God foreseen by the prophets has taken place (I Peter 1:10-12). What does this mean for the destiny of both the Old and the New Israel? for mankind as a whole? The old forces of strife and war are still at work. On what does the church found its certainty of victory? Where lies its hope?

Paul's Interpretation of History

The very calling of Paul as apostle to the Gentiles constrained him to ponder over God's ways. As a faithful Jew, Paul believed in the Lordship of God over all history. How then had God allowed his chosen People to reject him? Paul must have wrestled with this problem in deep agony of mind and soul. Out of this wrestling the letter to the Romans was born.

The letter to the Romans has been regarded since Luther's day as the letter which expounds the doctrine of justification by faith. Of course, this is true. Yet the scope of the letter is much wider than that. It gives us a total reinterpretation of history, the axis of world history being the coming of Christ in the flesh. The central theme of the letter might well be found in the eleventh chapter: " For God has consigned all men to disobedience, that he may have mercy upon all " (Rom. 11:32).

Paul starts his letter by showing that all mankind, Jews and Gentiles alike, are alienated from God. Adam is the archetype of mankind under the power of death. Abraham, through his faith in God's promise, becomes the father of all believers. But deliverance comes through Christ, the Second Adam, who takes all those who believe in him into his death and into his victory. Paul writes to the Corinthians: " The first man was from the earth, a man of dust; the second man is from heaven. . . . Just as we have borne the image of the man of dust, we shall also bear the image of the man of heaven." (I Cor. 15:47, 49.)

This new life in Christ is described in Rom., ch. 6: " Do you not know that all of us who have been baptized into Christ Jesus were baptized into his death? . . . So that as Christ was raised from the dead by the glory of the Father, we too might walk in newness of life." (Vs. 3-4.) The death of Christ is, if we may say so, a corporate act. The Son of Man represents mankind; he dies our death in order to have us participate in his life. This substitution of one for many, this participation in faith of the " many " as the act of one, is deeply rooted in the Hebrew tradition. We have seen how the young Hebrew was to consider the events of the exodus as a deliverance in which he himself participated, as something done to him and for him. Paul shares this conviction: "I want you to know . . . that our fathers were all under the cloud, and all passed through the sea." (I Cor. 10:1.) As the ancient People of God were baptized into Moses, so the new People of God are baptized into Christ, carried by him from death to life, from slavery to freedom. In both cases the oneness of the People thus formed rests on a common deliverance, on God's great act of mercy.

But there is a fundamental difference. The baptism into Moses called forth a relationship that materialized in obedience to the law. The baptism into Christ is a communication of the life of the risen Christ to the believer. A personal relationship is now established with God come in the flesh, the victorious Son of Man. We are no more under the law, but under the Spirit. The change of heart announced by Jeremiah and Ezekiel has occurred. We are made sons of God by participation in the life of the Son. A captive mankind now tastes the glorious liberty of the children of God. Romans, ch. 8, is Christianity's great hymn of deliverance.

This chapter shows the new life of the Spirit as a God-given, present reality. Faith is not " pious wishing "; it is an active and dynamic power at work in those who stake their all on Christ and live not according to the flesh but by the Spirit (see Rom. 8:1–17). We should always remember that for Paul the " flesh " means not our physical body but our Adamic fallen nature — body and soul — as over against the life from above of those who are redeemed by Christ, body and soul. While offering this power to live by the Spirit, Paul well knows of the tension between the new creature striving to be born and the old Adam. Not only we men, but the whole creation, yearns for the glorious liberty of the children of God. This yearning is compared to the travail of childbirth. We wait for our adoption as sons and this is the hope by which we live (Rom. 8:18–25).

We see in this chapter the whole tension of the church-between-the-times, belonging in faith to the world to come which has already broken in, yet still living in the old world. " Already — not yet." The new certainty of this hope as com-

pared with that of the prophets is that the decisive victory has
already been won by Christ on the cross. He who has called us
to be conformed to the image of his Son will achieve what he
has begun. His faithfulness to the eternal purpose unfolded in
Christ is our security. This is why Rom., ch. 8, can end in a
hymn of victory.

But, if God's election is the basis of our security, what about
those in Israel who have rejected him? Can God take back his
word? No, never. His promises hold. And Paul, in chs. 9 to 11,
develops the thought that Israel's rejection is temporary: it is
meant to open the door of salvation to the non-Jews. The day
will come when God's promise will come true and Zion will
know its Redeemer. Then it will know the breadth and depth
of God's mercy. All pride will be reduced to nought. Pagans
and Jews will both have learned the miracle of salvation by
grace. This is the ultimate meaning and goal of the long drama
of history.

Chapters 9 to 11 of Romans are also meant as a warning to
the newborn communities grafted on the old stem of Israel. If
the old branches have been broken off, the new ones might be
broken off too. No guarantee of perennial existence is given
to the historical churches. They too can be rejected, they can
wither and die. All we know is that God's plan cannot be
thwarted, even by human unfaithfulness. He will not leave himself without witnesses. He will lead history to its ultimate fulfillment.

We have seen already, in Rom., ch. 8, that not only mankind
but creation as a whole is eagerly waiting for the revelation of
the sons of God. This thought of a cosmic deliverance and renewal, of a new creation, is expressed in I Cor., ch. 15, and
further developed in Ephesians and Colossians. Christ's redeeming activity will go on until " he has put all his enemies under
his feet " (I Cor. 15:25), the last enemy to be destroyed being
death. God has entrusted all things to the Son for his great work

of reconciliation. "When all things are subjected to him, then the Son himself will also be subjected to him who put all things under him, that God may be everything to every one." (I Cor. 15:28.) The ultimate goal of history is communion with God and our fellow men: the free response of love to love.

The King and Judge of mankind is he who stooped down and took the form of a servant. The words of Paul to the Philippians, possibly quoted from an ancient hymn, are perhaps the most impressive Christological statement of the whole New Testament. But they are not first and foremost a piece of Christological doctrine; they are meant to convey to the Philippians what it means for a Christian community to be conformed to Christ (Phil. 2:5-11). The downward movement of God in Christ is the counterpart of the upward movement of the first Adam. It is the movement of self-giving love as over against the willful self-assertion (see Gen. 3:5; 11:4: "Let us make a name for ourselves").

Christ is not only the center of Biblical revelation, the center of human history. He is also its end and its beginning. For it is in him that the destiny of mankind receives its meaning and finds its fulfillment, according to the eternal purpose of God. "There is one God, the Father, from whom are all things and for whom we exist." (I Cor. 8:6.) From the beginning of time God has seen us and willed us to be in Christ. He is manhood in its full stature, the true image of the invisible God. In him our human existence finds its real destiny. Through him we are saved. In him we live, to God's praise and glory. This is the vision of history conveyed to us in the letters to the Colossians and to the Ephesians.

But this vision again transcends the destiny of mankind. It embraces the universe. "For in him all things were created, in heaven and on earth, visible and invisible, whether thrones or dominions or principalities or authorities — all things were created through him and for him. He is before all things, and in him all things hold together. . . . For in him all the fullness of God was pleased to dwell, and through him to reconcile to himself all things, whether on earth or in heaven, making peace by the blood of his cross." (Col. 1:16–17, 19–20; see Eph., ch. 1.) The death of Christ has cosmic significance. Not only has the bond which condemned mankind been "nailed to the cross" and canceled. The principalities and powers which claim to rule this world have been disarmed and conquered. (Col. 2: 14–15. In New Testament language the "powers" seem to be both heavenly beings controlling the affairs of this world and the earthly authorities influenced by them.)

Again — as in Romans — this affirmation does not mean that the world is no longer in the grip of adverse powers. But Christ's victory means that the rule of these powers is temporary. God's redeeming grace has reduced to nought the *ultimate claim* of all other "powers" and "authorities." In a suggestive image Professor Cullmann has compared our situation to that of the Allies between D Day and V Day: the country is still occupied and there can be fierce battles ahead, but the occupying power is doomed and knows it. The decisive battle is won and the issue is certain. (*Christ and Time.* The Westminster Press, 1950.)

Do we not in the church sometimes lack this note of triumphant certainty which runs through the apostolic message? Do we not allow ourselves to be too impressed by the temporary victories of fleeting powers of this world, whatever their name?

John's View of History

For John the decisive hour of world history is "the hour" of Christ's twofold elevation on the cross and in glory, these two events being fundamentally one. The whole ministry of Jesus is focused on this hour. For this hour has he come. In this hour the ruler of this world is to be cast out. Through being lifted up on the cross Christ will draw all men to himself and thus glorify God. (See John 12:27–33; see also chs. 3:14; 8:28; 13:1; 17:1.)

While the Son of Man is condemned on earth, another trial takes place in the court of God. There the great accuser is cast out, while the Son is justified, and with him all those who believe in him. (On this point we owe a great deal to Theo Preiss's essay on " Justification in Johannine Thought," in his book *Life in Christ*. S. C. M. Press, Ltd., London, 1954.) The Holy Spirit is the witness who convinces the world "of sin and of righteousness and of judgment " (John 16:8). The decisive hour for every man is the hour of his encounter with Christ: it is a matter of turning to the light or preferring darkness. We thus pronounce God's judgment on us. We are measured, we remain enslaved or are made free, according to our attitude to the Son of Man, our rejecting or receiving his word. (See John, chs. 3:16–21; 8:31–32; 12:44–50.) For he is the true Son of Man and Son of God. He is " the Word made flesh." The spoken word of God, which we have heard ringing all through the Old Testament, is now embodied in a man's life. God's holy will is done. God's self-giving love is manifested: " He who has seen me has seen the Father " (John 14:9). " No one takes it [my life] from me, but I lay it down of my own accord." (John 10:18.) The oneness of the Son and the Father is a perfect oneness in will and purpose. And this purpose is the salvation of the world.

As God is light, so the Son is " the light of the world " (John 8:1). As God is life, so the Son is the life-giver, " the bread of life " (see John 6:35). His solemn "I am " is a direct echo of the " I am " of the Old Testament. Truth is no more a concept, it is the truth of a life lived by a man among men. " Here is the man! " (John 19:5.) The evangelist certainly intentionally quotes this word of Pilate as having a deeper meaning.

The Son of Man comes from above. The Fourth Gospel affirms the pre-existence of the Son of Man: a concept familiar to Jewish circles (John, chs. 3:13; 8:58; see also Dan. 7:13–14 and the Book of Enoch, which appears to have exerted a great influence on Jewish thinking at the time of Jesus. In this work, the

Son of Man is pre-existent, he is to come as judge at the end of time, and he is to reign over the whole cosmos).

To believe in Christ means to be born again — born from above (John, chs. 3:3; 5:21–29). For him who abides in Christ, life eternal has already begun. He has already undergone judgment and met divine forgiveness. This has led some scholars to the belief that for John the Parousia (the final manifestation of Christ) has already taken place with his resurrection and the coming of the Spirit (see for instance C. H. Dodd, *The Interpretation of the Fourth Gospel*, p. 395, etc., Cambridge University Press, 1953). We believe that the living tension between the " already " and the " not yet " that we found in Paul is also present in John. It is true that the main stress lies on the actual presence of Christ through the Spirit. But this does not exclude a firm expectation of Christ's coming in power and might on the Last Day as King and Judge (see John, chs. 5:28–29; 6:40). The tension is expressed in clear words in The First Letter of John: " Beloved, we are God's children now; it does not yet appear what we shall be, but we know that when he appears we shall be like him, for we shall see him as he is. And every one who thus hopes in him purifies himself as he is pure."

When our Lord in his last discourse compared the sorrow of his disciples to that of a woman in travail, he may have thought of the dark days ahead between his death and his resurrection. But surely he knew that both the anguish and the joy of childbearing would go on for his church to the end of time until the new creation comes to life (see John 16:21–22).

In quite different language, John presents us with an interpretation of history which is the same, in all essentials, as Paul's. Of this history Christ is the beginning, the center, and the goal.

John the Seer

The little apocalypses of the Gospels had already warned the church that there is no smooth path to the Kingdom of God.

Strife and persecution were looming ahead. The last struggle would be the hardest. Many would fall away: " Most men's love will grow cold." (Matt. 24:12.) When this twenty-fourth chapter of Matthew was written down, the blood of martyrs had already been spilled in Nero's Rome. Jerusalem had been destroyed in A.D. 70.

It is on a similar background that we must see and interpret the book of Revelation. Once more the very life of the church is threatened, and it is in danger of forsaking the " love [it] . . . had at first" (Rev. 2:4). The most widely accepted date for the book of Revelation is the reign of Domitian around the year 95. Emperor worship was enforced throughout the Empire, which for the Christians meant apostasy or martyrdom. This explains the cryptic character of the book. The modern reader, not familiar with the terminology of Jewish apocalyptic, is puzzled by this wealth of symbols and images. But this should not hide from us the fundamental message of the book: above the earthly rulers there is a higher Ruler: CHRISTUS IMPERATOR.

Christ appears to the exile on a Sunday morning in imperial array and majesty: "Fear not, I am the first and the last, and the living one; I died, and behold I am alive for evermore, and I have the keys of Death and Hades." (Rev. 1:17–18.) Here is one greater than Caesar. The final word belongs to the " King of kings " (Rev. 19:16). Blessed are those who will remain faithful to the end, those who have not been led astray! For many in the church " have the name of being alive, and . . . are dead " (Rev. 3:1).

The Seer stands at the gates of heaven. He is introduced to the divine liturgy sung by the celestial choirs to the glory of God Almighty. He is shown a scroll where the destiny of mankind is written. He weeps, for the scroll is sealed. It is then revealed to him that one only can open the scroll: the Lion of Judah, the Root of David; for he has conquered. " And between the throne and the four living creatures and among the elders,

I saw a Lamb standing, as though it had been slain." (Rev. 5:6.) It is the slain Lamb of God who holds the keys of history. And it is those who suffer with him who shall reign with him.

In a series of startling visions the Seer is shown the powers of evil let loose in the world. The end has not yet come. But the Lord puts his seal on his own. The days of the " Beast " are numbered; its downfall will be as great as has been its power; its power will be reduced to nought forever. The bloody imagery of the last chapters of the book seems weird to the Christian mind. The message it is meant to convey, however, is clear. It is the condemnation of the totalitarian state which claims what belongs to God alone — namely, the souls of men. And it is a great affirmation of faith: God himself, in his own day, will put an end to all injustice, and destroy the powers of sin and death which hold humanity captive.

In a last vision we are shown the new Jerusalem coming down from heaven in radiant beauty as a bride adorned for her bridegroom. The old prophecies are fulfilled, a new heaven and a new earth have come into being, and God " tabernacles " among men. God's glory is the City's light and the Lamb is its flame. " By its light shall the nations walk; and the kings of the earth shall bring their glory into it." (Rev. 21:24; see also Isa., chs. 60:1–3, 19–20; 65:17–19.) The river of the water of life flows now from the throne of God and of the Lamb, bright as crystal, and the leaves of the tree of life are " for the healing of the nations " (Rev. 22:2; see also Ezek., ch. 47; Gen., chs. 2:10; 3:22–23).

This is no abstract world of spirits, it is a world throbbing with life, into which all the gifts of " the nations " will be brought to the glory of God. And the power that brings this new creation into being is the divine power of vicarious love.

CHAPTER XII

The Church " Between the Times "

" That the world may believe." (John 17:21.)

We have seen the apostolic church looking forward to its consummation. It stands under the twofold sign of Christ's resurrection and of his coming again in glory and might. It stands
between the times: its citizenship is in heaven, its task is on
earth. What does this mean for its daily life? How will the tension between these two worlds manifest itself? What does it
mean for the church of Christ to be " in " and not " of " the
world? What bearing will its faith in the Lordship of Christ
have on social ethics as well as on personal behavior? What
guidance can we find in its teaching for our own life and witness in the twentieth century?

We shall not attempt to solve such wide and complex questions in one brief closing chapter. All we can do is to open some
lines of thought.

Sign and Token

The church is seen in the whole New Testament as a new
society which, in an alien world, is a sign and token of the
Kingdom to come. By the Spirit operating in and through it,
it belongs to the world to come. Made of men whose redemption is still a reality waited and hoped for (see Rom. 8:22–25),
it belongs to the present era, it shares in the sins of this world.

The tension of this twofold divine and human nature marks its whole historical existence. It is "holy," set apart for the service of God, sanctified by Christ. Yet it is still in the grip of the adversary, whose divisive work operates not only from without but from within, seeking to distort or destroy its witnessing function in the world.

Thus it is constantly to be reminded of its calling. For it is meant to be an exemplary society, a challenge to the surrounding world. Its life is to be based on an attitude that is in fundamental opposition to the current standards of the world: "The kings of the Gentiles exercise lordship over them; and those in authority over them are called benefactors. But not so with you; rather let the greatest among you become as the youngest, and the leader as one who serves" (Luke 22:25-26; see also Mark 10:42-45). Not domination, but service; not pride, but humility; not self-defense, but hatred overcome by love; duplicity and lust overcome by singleness of heart: such are the new commandments laid down by the Lord of the church. And he has lived them. Therefore, the call of the apostles is a call to be conformed to Christ as over against being conformed to the world. This is the basic principle of all church ethics. (See Rom. 12:1-2; Phil. 2:5; I Peter, chs. 1:13-17; 2:11-12.)

Two concepts illustrate this and will be studied now more closely: the Petrine concept of the People of God and the Pauline concept of the church as Christ's body on earth.

The New People of God

The First Letter of Peter takes up the very words of Ex., ch. 19, and applies them to the church. This lays stress first of all on the continuity between the Old and the New Israel. As Old Israel was set apart to be God's "own possession; . . . a kingdom of priests . . . a holy nation," so the New Israel is to be "a chosen race, a royal priesthood, a holy nation, God's own people" (Ex. 19:5-6; I Peter 2:9; see also I Peter 2:5; on Ex., ch. 19, see Ch. III). In the Old Israel, the claim of the sovereign God was on the total life of his people. Such is his claim on his church. There cannot be a reserved sphere governed by other rules, a secular versus a religious life, a Sunday versus an everyday religion. There cannot be cleric versus lay, with varying standards. Every Christian participates in the holy priesthood of his Lord and Savior. Every Christian is to offer " spiritual sacrifices " — a dedicated life. Every Christian is to proclaim God's " wonderful deeds " and to bear witness in word and deed as Christ's ambassador in and to the world (see I Peter 2:10; II Cor. 5:14–20).

There is one point on which the New Israel differs from the Old: the new " race " is in no sense an ethical or geographical entity. It is a race born from above, a nation whose citizenship is in heaven. The church of God is a pilgrim People marching toward the Kingdom of which the Promised Land was a sign and a symbol (see I Peter 1:17; Heb., chs. 11:8–16; 13:14). This means that the church is universal by the very nature of its calling. It is a brotherhood sealed with the blood of its Lord and Savior. There is a priority of our belonging to God's People over all other allegiances based on family ties, class interests, or nationality.

The integration of Jews and Gentiles in the one church of Christ was a tremendous event which came as a shock to the Palestinian Christians of Jewish origin. We know what a fierce battle Paul had to fight when he declared that the Gentiles were saved by Christ alone and need not submit to the Jewish law. This was essentially a theological issue, but it had far-reaching consequences for the universality of the church. " For as many of you as were baptized into Christ have put on Christ. There is neither Jew nor Greek, there is neither slave nor free, there is neither male nor female; for you are all one in Christ Jesus. And if you are Christ's, then you are Abraham's offspring, heirs according to promise." (Gal. 3:27–29.)

Here again the continuity with the Old Israel is stressed; for the true succession acknowledged by Christ and by the apostolic church is that of faith. All heirs of the Kingdom! This is the common status of God's People, and it would be strange indeed that those who are to sit together at the celestial banquet should not sit at the same table on earth! (See Matt. 8:10–11; Eph. 2:13–22.)

How often in the history of the church has national, racial, or social prejudice gained the upper hand! Is not nationalism one of the most dangerous and subtle idols of the modern world? We like to believe that the problem was less acute in Jesus' time, but this is not true. Jesus stood in the feverish atmosphere of the Zealot movement, and lost his popularity by taking a firm stand against the Zealots. He stressed the primacy of the Kingdom of God in unequivocal terms, and the apostles followed his lead.

Are we not constrained to ask ourselves whether the very existence of " national " churches is not a denial of the vocation of the one church of God on earth? The church on earth is submitted, it is true, to limitations of time and space. It shares the life and concerns, the cultural background, of the people among whom it stands as God's witness. This is a condition for an effective communication of the gospel, the very law of incarnation. The betrayal begins when the national churches claim total autonomy; when they allow the standards and categories of the world to take the upper hand over their own; when national, racial, or social prejudice invades them; when the ideologies and slogans of the world blur the one message they have to proclaim throughout the ages: " Christ crucified, a stumblingblock to Jews and folly to Gentiles." (I Cor. 1:23.) A church living in isolation is in constant danger of losing sight of the absolute primacy of God's claim over all earthly claims, and of the fullness of the gospel. We all need to be strengthened and called to order by our sister churches all over the world.

The Body of Christ

The image of the body brings in a new element because it stresses the *organic* character of the relation between Christ and his church, and of the members of the church with one another. Let us examine some of the implications of this figure.

First, the body is our medium of communication with the outer world. To reveal God's will on earth, Christ took a body (Heb. 10:5-9). To say that we are his body is to say that the church is the place where God's will is now to be revealed, where the life of Christ is to be manifested in word and deed. It is to be his voice, his healing hands, his wandering feet. He has chosen to work through it, he has delegated to it the power he has received from his Father: "He who receives you receives me, and he who receives me receives him who sent me." (Matt. 10:40.) "Truly, I say to you, whatever you bind on earth shall be bound in heaven." (Matt. 18:18.) "As the Father has sent me, even so I send you." (John 20:21.)

It is to the immediate disciples, and through them to the whole church as a body, that Christ speaks these words which fill us with awe. The responsibility of representing him and speaking in his name lies on the fellowship of the believers.

Secondly, the body is an organic unity which cannot be divided without damage to the whole. Life flows from the stem to the branches, from the head to the members. Christ is the vine, he is the body. We are incorporated in him. A branch cut off withers and dies. A member cut off ceases to exist. To belong to Christ is to belong to his church. In the perspective of the New Testament, a Christian living in isolation is unthinkable — a contradiction in terms.

Again, the life of the body implies diversity in unity. This is Paul's dominant thought in both Rom., ch. 12, and I Cor., chs. 12 to 14. There are many gifts and corresponding functions. God is the giver. Therefore, no one can pride himself on his gifts nor disregard the gifts of others. And fullness of life is attained only when all members of the body are healthy and contribute to the life of the whole.

We are here given some precious indications as to the life and structure of the church. There is a diversity of ministries, that is, of "services." If there is a hierarchy of functions, it can only be according to the measure of the Spirit that God bestows. Those who are leaders should consider themselves as those who serve, in all humility and love. (See Rom. 12:3–11; I Cor. 12:4–31; Luke 22:26.) And of all gifts, the greatest — without which all others are of no avail — is love. This is the recurring note in all the apostolic letters, as in the saying of Jesus himself. (See I Cor., ch. 13; Phil. 2:1–8; I John, chs. 3:14–18; 4:7–12; John 13:34.)

The very insistence of these letters on "mutual subjection," on forbearance, each counting others better than himself and seeking their interest rather than his own (Eph. 5:21; Phil. 2:3–4), shows that failure to fulfill the law of love has been one of the stumbling blocks of Christian communities from the very beginning. But it was also considered as the decisive test of their discipleship. The danger of taking pride in one's own gifts while disregarding those of others was always looming on the horizon, as is shown by the chaotic assemblies at Corinth. Paul firmly reminds the churches that "God is not a God of confusion but of peace" (I Cor. 14:33; see also the entire chapter). Every gift must be used for the building up of the church.

Furthermore, the unity of the church is seen at the same time both as something given and as a goal to be attained. Unity belongs to the very essence of the church! "There is one body and one Spirit, . . . one hope . . . one Lord, one faith, one baptism, one God and Father of us all, who is above all and through all and in all." (Eph. 4:4–6.) The passage is probably referring to the unity of Jews and Gentiles, but the truth it states remains the same for the church throughout the world. It is not in our power to make the church one, for its unity is God-given. We can only *manifest* this unity in word and deed. In fact, the church has still to be "built up," "until we all attain to the unity of the faith and of the knowledge of the Son of God, to mature manhood, to the measure of the stature of the fullness of Christ; so that we may no longer be children, tossed to and fro and carried about with every wind of doctrine" (Eph. 4:12–14). This growth is to be a growth in the truth and a growth in love. Only thus can we attain "mature manhood" in Christ.

Looking at our churches we must humbly confess that we are still "babes in the faith," "tossed to and fro," and divided. Is it not, at least, one of the gifts of the Spirit to this century that we have become more acutely aware of the sin of division and of the stumbling block these divisions place on the path of all missionary endeavor? The unity our Lord prayed for is no less than the perfect unity of the Father and the Son. This unity should not be understood, first of all, as "mystical." The nurture of the Son is to do the Father's will and to achieve his purpose. Our oneness with Christ and with one another is the condition to be fulfilled if the world is to believe in him.

It is the "otherness" and "oneness" of the church as a community governed by the Spirit, it is the quality of its fellowship, that alone can convince a skeptical world, tired of words, of the truth of its message, of the reality of God's power and mercy.

Church Ethics and Social Structures

The basis of all Christian ethics is God's redeeming act in Christ. After expounding God's plan of salvation in Rom., chs. 1 to 11, Paul continues, "I appeal to you *therefore,* brethren . . ." (Rom. 12:1). This little word "therefore" marks the transition between what God has done and what we are called to be and to do (see Eph., chs. 2:11; 4:1; 5:1; Phil. 2:12). Our behavior toward our brother is determined by the knowledge that Christ died for him (see Rom. 14:15; I Cor. 8:9–12). Liberty is limited by love, by the regard we must have for God's will to save all men. We have already seen how this redeeming purpose cuts across all barriers of race, sex, or social status (see Gal. 3:25–28; Col. 3:1–11). We have " put on the new nature, which is being renewed in knowledge after the image of its creator . . . Christ is all, and in all " (Col. 3:10–11). Could any statement be more revolutionary? All forgiven sinners living by the same grace! All in process of being transformed into the likeness of Christ. Earthly distinctions are reduced to nought.

And yet the apostolic church is careful not to draw from such a statement the social consequences it seems to imply. When it turns to practical problems such as marriage, slavery, or politics, the rules laid down sound strangely conservative to modern ears! Why is this so?

It is a delicate undertaking to deal in a few lines with such a controversial matter. But we cannot avoid raising the question, because it is at this point that the problem of church vs. world comes up in an acute form. Did Paul's or Peter's social ethics simply conform to the customs and prejudices of the time? Should we consider their views as time-bound? Or is there in the position they take some underlying truth permanently valid for all times? Their "conservatism" has been a stumbling block for many forward-looking Christians, all the more so because throughout the centuries other Christians have used Scriptural references to legitimate the old class system, slavery, subordination of women, unconditional obedience to the state, and so on.

Before discussing specific problems, we shall venture some general remarks concerning the theological convictions on which the attitude of the church was based and the conditions in which it lived.

For one thing, the affirmation stated in Rom., ch. 13, that "there is no authority except from God, and those that exist have been instituted by God" (v. 1) is certainly the guiding conviction which determines Paul's attitude, not only to the state, but also to what he considers a God-willed hierarchy in the family and in the relation of master to servant. But this means, first of all, that God is the sovereign Ruler and that every authority functioning in the world is a delegated authority. The person in authority is answerable to God; the person under authority should obey as obeying God himself. Both are placed before a higher and final claim. God wills an ordered life without which life in society becomes impossible. We are to pray for our rulers "that we may lead a quiet and peaceable life" (I Tim. 2:2). The thought in I Peter is the same: "Be subject for the Lord's sake to every human institution. . . . Fear God. Honor the emperor" (ch. 2:13, 17). These last words are significant: only God must be *feared;* his judgment is the only one that really matters. But the human authorities set up by God should, as such, be respected. This is the attitude the apostles took toward the Roman Empire — a pagan state, but a state that insures at least a minimum of law and order. The same rule prevails in the household. Both the one who commands and those who obey should do so "in the Lord," remembering that they have a Master in heaven to whom they will give account for their behavior (see Col. 3:18 to 4:1 also Eph. 6:1–9).

The principle that one should see the authority of God behind all human authorities sets the *limit* of human obedience. Jesus had definitely stated the primacy of his call over all other allegiances, even — humanly speaking — the most sacred (Matt. 10:32–39; Mark 13:12–13; Luke 9:59–62). And in telling his disciples to give to Caesar what was Caesar's and to God what was God's, he made clear that we cannot give to Caesar what belongs to God (Mark 12:13–17). Therefore, when emperor worship was enforced, all faithful Christians accepted martyrdom rather than deny their Lord.

A second decisive theological conviction of the early church was that in following the way of the Master, Christians would bear witness to their God in the pagan world. This way had been one of nonresistance to violence. Christ had acknowledged Pilate's authority as from God. He had forgiven his enemies. He had been obedient unto death (John 19:11; Luke, chs. 22:42; 23:34; Heb. 5:7-10). He had surmounted evil by the sole power of forbearing love. Judgment was to be left to God. The exhortations of Paul in Rom. 12:17-21 are a direct echo of the Sermon on the Mount.

It is in accepting the conditions in which God has placed us, those which were ours when we were "found," that we shall bear the most effective witness to the new life bestowed upon us. (See I Cor. 7:17-24. Verse 21 can be interpreted in two ways, and there is disagreement among scholars whether the opportunity to be seized is to gain freedom or to stay a slave.) And it is this witness that matters. The slave will witness his acquired freedom if he obeys even an unjust master "as to the Lord." For the freedom he enjoys is freedom from sin — from all scorn and hatred, from all willful self-assertion. This point is stressed again and again in I Peter. Christ has suffered unjustly, hence we should be ready to show our genuine discipleship by willingly accepting suffering at the hand of men (I Peter, chs. 2:18-25; 3:1-2, 9-22; 4:1-7, 12-19). The end is near, and God will judge the living and the dead. The central concern all through is one of personal witness, of faithfulness to the Lord. The problem of social justice is not raised. But those who practice injustice are reminded of an ultimate judgment.

For similar reasons, Paul blames those who go to law "before the unrighteous instead of the saints" (see I Cor. 6:1-8; Matt. 18:15-17). In the course of history, Christians have all too often taken the weapons of the world to defend their personal rights, or the rights of the church. We have indulged in "holy crusades." That this is contrary to the example of Jesus and to the teaching of the apostolic church is beyond discussion.

Yet the other side of the question remains to be faced: Why do we find in the apostolic letters no criticism of existing social and political structures? The prudence of the church in these matters is in striking contrast with the teaching of the prophets. We believe that besides the motives already mentioned, there are three reasons for this attitude:

First, the nearness of the end. The first generation of Christians believed that this world was going to disappear in their lifetime. To proclaim the gospel was therefore urgent.

Secondly, any interference with existing social and political structures would have exposed the Christian communities to the accusation of being insurrectional, a threat to the unity and safety of the Empire. We have seen that Jesus himself, in spite of his clear position, had been condemned as a political leader. It is significant that the New Testament writers insist on the responsibility of the Jews in the condemnation of Jesus and minimize the role of the Roman authorities (see Acts, chs. 4:10; 5:30; 10:39). Paul is always the victim of the Jews; he enjoys the protection of Roman authorities. We do not mean that this is not true, but it seems to be intentionally stressed. Great efforts are made to prove that the Christians are loyal citizens of the Empire. In fact, they are under constant suspicion, and persecutions finally break out. A totalitarian state soon comes to suspect the church because it acknowledges an authority higher than that of the state and is capable of resisting unto death where its soul is threatened. It wants, however, to suffer for the right motive.

Thirdly, the spiritual revolution we have described above is so fundamental that where it is understood and carried out, human relationships are basically changed. The seed is sown, which will bear fruit in its own time. The church, therefore, rather than being revolutionary, was willing to sow the seed of social change through the gospel, cultivate it through its teaching, and patiently await the harvest.

Two Concrete Examples

Let us illustrate what has just been said by two concrete examples: The Letter of Paul to Philemon about his runaway slave, and Paul's attitude toward women.

Legally Philemon is in his right and Onesimus is wrong. Paul does not question this. He declares himself ready to pay Onesimus' debts. But how movingly the apostle pleads the case of the slave. Onesimus is " his child." Philemon has lost a slave, he recovers " a beloved brother." He should receive the runaway slave as he would receive the apostle himself, as a " partner " in the service of God. Could a relationship be more utterly changed, whatever the future status of Onesimus may have been?

As to women, Paul has often been charged with having an " antiwoman complex." Nothing seems to us more absurd. His advocacy of celibacy in I Cor. 7:25-35 is presented as a personal opinion, and is based solely on the seriousness of the times and the urgency of the missionary task, which requires a maximum of freedom from earthly cares. Several women were numbered among his active co-workers. The way in which he appreciated their help, as well as his regard for them, might well be given as an example to some modern churches where the ministry of women is still considered as of little importance (see Rom. 16:1-4, 6, 13, 15).

By stating that in Christ there is neither male nor female, Paul has expressed the fundamental equality of men and women as heirs of the same promise. From a Jewish point of view this was a revolutionary thought! While circumcision was the sacramental act by which men entered the old covenant, through baptism men and women alike enter the new covenant, and share the same status in the universal priesthood of all believers.

Behind this new status given to women by the church, we must see the attitude of Jesus himself. He deals with them as persons, worthy to be talked to and listened to, in need of salvation equally with men. The freedom of Jesus in his encounters with women puzzled not only the Pharisees but the disciples themselves (see Luke 7:36–49; John 4:27). He found among them his most humble listeners; in them he met with the deepest gratitude. The story of the anointing in Bethany seems to show that a woman was the only one to have a foreboding of his Passion. All four Gospels testify that he made women the first witnesses and heralds of his resurrection. Pastor Westphal, in a report on the ministry of women to the National Synod of the French Reformed Church, interprets the three Marys of the Gospels as symbolic of the threefold vocation of the church: as the "handmaiden" of the Lord (Luke 1:38), the "listening" church (Luke 10:39–42), and the "proclaiming" church (Luke 24:10). Of the ministries enumerated in I Cor., ch. 12, we know that women exercised that of prophecy (considered at the time as one of the highest), that of helper, that of hospitality, and probably that of instruction and cure of souls. (Besides Rom., ch. 16, see Acts 21:9; I Cor. 11:5; Acts, chs. 16:13–15; 18:26.)

Over against these facts, however, we must see the other side of the picture. For one thing, Paul is anxious for women to submit themselves to the accepted customs of their time. This is a matter both of dignity and decency. (See I Cor., chs. 11:3–16; 14:34–35; Col. 3:18–19; I Tim. 2:9–15.) It seems to us that one should retain the spirit, not the letter, of such advice. Customs change; but every sensitive woman will feel, I believe, that what Paul wants to preserve is something of the essence of womanhood, her dignity and reserve.

The second matter raises an even more controversial and delicate issue. Paul considers the subordination of the married woman to her husband as part of the order of creation. He maintains firmly the principle of a God-given hierarchy within the family: the husband's authority over the wife, the parents' authority over the children (see Col. 3:18–21; Eph. 6:1–4). At the same time, here again the relationship is put in a quite new light. Husband and wife belong to one another, and each one rules over the body of the other (I Cor. 7:3–4). In a most significant passage, Eph. 5:21–33, the wife in her relation to her husband is a figure of the church, as the husband in his relation to his wife is a figure of Christ. What does this mean? It indicates that the husband carries the responsibility of leadership in the family, but his attitude is to be conformed to that of Christ, who came as a servant and gave his life for his church. The wife is the dependent and receptive one, but in this she exemplifies, by the very nature of her vocation, the calling of the church as a whole (men and women alike) to be Christ's servant. And the whole passage begins with a call to mutual subjection addressed to all Christians. Could the conception of marriage be lifted to a higher level than this?

We have dealt at some length with the couple because it is the cell of the community and exemplifies certain characteristics of all true community in Christ. Let us now summarize our findings: (1) A Christian community is a community under the Lord; whether man or woman, master or servant, all stand under one sovereign authority; (2) all share in the same grace and the same promise, and this constitutes their fundamental equality; (3) God is a God of order; each one is therefore assigned his or her proper place, with a view to the harmonious development of the whole; (4) the one who rules should be as the one who serves, and the one who serves should rejoice in his or her service; (5) self-giving love is the common rule, for God is love; (6) it is by such a life lived in conformity to Christ that the community — the home, the parish, the church at large — reveals to the world the true nature of community living.

Then and Now

We have tried to sketch the history of God's People over a span of about two thousand years. Since then, nearly another two thousand years have gone by, and another story might be written! In some ways, the twofold temptation of the church remains the same throughout the centuries: the temptation to conform to the world — the salt losing its savor, therefore becoming useless; and the temptation to live in self-contented isolation — the salt kept in the salt bag, again useless.

It has been said of the twentieth century that it would be "the century of the church." In some ways this is true. The ecumenical movement and the laymen's movements springing up in so many countries are concrete signs that the Spirit is at work in this generation, and that the church is awakening to a new consciousness of its task throughout the world and in all spheres of life. At the same time, forces hostile to Christianity have grown in strength and scope. In a number of countries minority churches are struggling for their existence. In others, outward success may be enticing the church to drift along unconsciously in the comforts of the present life and to become this-worldly in the wrong sense. We are still a "stiff-necked people" running after other gods — only the name of these gods has slightly changed.

The call of the hour is to *be* the church. We have seen what it means: a People that proclaim by word and deed the sovereign Lordship of Christ and the power of his resurrection; a free People whose treasure cannot be taken away from them by earthly powers, and who look beyond the crisis of history to its final consummation. A distraught and despairing world is in need of this firm word of faith and hope. At the same time, God's People must stand with both feet on the ground, in the everyday "here and now" assigned to them by their particular calling. They must do this not only as individual members of a family or a congregation, or as members of a certain profession, but also as responsible citizens of a given country, set in the wider context of a world of nations.

It is on this point that our situation differs from that of the first century. We are answerable, together with our fellow men, for the evils of the society within which we live. Here the message of the prophets of old will complete that of the apostolic church. The prophets lived responsibly in the turmoil of history, proclaiming relentlessly the Lord's judgment on all unrighteousness and his mercy on those who repent and believe. We are not "prophets"; but we have to project the clear light of God's word on the conditions of our time. We must try to go, as the prophets did, to the roots of evil. This often implies working for changes in existing structures in the social as well as the political sphere.

This is, we believe, the "prophetic" task of the church. It is set as a watchman over the city to denounce unrighteousness, to defend the defenseless, to remind the state of its mission to maintain law and order. It is to help its laymen to work effectively in their respective spheres for a better order, for only the specialist can unravel the intricacies of modern industry, trade, and politics and suggest constructive solutions. The Bible offers no ready-made blueprints that we can follow; there lies our difficulty. Its ethics are not static, but dynamic; they are not a set of rules, but a demand for concrete obedience to the Lord of the church here and now, in every new situation. Every generation, in communion with the long chain of witnesses who have preceded it and under the guidance of the same Spirit, must grasp anew the tasks that the Lord of the church sets before it. What the Bible offers is a vision of God's saving purpose for man and society. It presents us with an ongoing dialogue between God and his People. It is in listening to this dialogue, humbly, prayerfully, steadily, that God's Word spoken to other generations in other circumstances, will become a living Word to the men and women of *this* generation in *their* circumstances. For his Word passeth not.

"He who has an ear, let him hear what the Spirit says to the churches." (Rev. 3:22.)